When will I be good enough?

When will I be good enough?

A REPLACEMENT CHILD'S JOURNEY TO HEALING

Barbara Jaffe, Ed.D.

LISA HAGAN BOOKS

To Paul, for the gift of his unconditional love

To my remarkable sons, Michael, Adam, and Brian, for their caring and patient hearts

To my sweet Emma, for her silent devotion as she lay on my lap while I wrote.

And…

With love and gratitude for Jeffrey, my brother whom I never met but have always known

There are two kinds of suffering. There is the suffering you run away from, which follows you everywhere. And there is the suffering you face directly, and in doing so become free.—Ajahn Chah

Author's Note:

When Will I Be Good Enough? A Replacement Child's Journey to Healing reflects my unique position in life, having been born into a family soon after my brother Jeffrey, the second child, died. My role as the replacement child, reinforced by my mother, who was never able to come to terms with her two-year old's sudden death, has greatly affected all areas of my life. However, my story is not about blame but observation—to focus on elements of my self-esteem, self-worth, and self-confidence, which were compromised. Through my journey of honest reflection and observation, I describe how I have learned to put myself back together, in a sense, to live a beautifully full and honorable life. While this book was written by a replacement child, it will help to heal someone whose life has been affected by an alcoholic, a depressed parent, a detached parent, or an abusive parent. We can recover from the disappointment and challenges we acquire in being raised by such parents. We can flourish!

Table of Contents

Preface

"Careful the things you say, children will listen." These powerful words from the musical *Into the Woods* go to the heart of the matter in describing the delicate and precarious interaction between parents and their children. Children are not blank slates as had once been thought. Quite the contrary, children are born with their own temperament which strongly influences their disposition and developing personality. But often this unfolding personality is highjacked because of early programming and parental intervention. *When Will I Be Good Enough? A Replacement Child's Journey to Healing* is Barbara Jaffe's beautiful rendering of such a story—one that poignantly shows us what can happen when the influence of a beloved parent changes the course of a young person's life; alters the way a child sees and learns to move through the world.

There are so many layers to this book. Any one of us can relate to the parent-child dynamic. Many of us feel misunderstood by those we feel should know us best of all—our parents. Children often feel as if they are not seen and heard for who they are in their own right. The theme of not being truly known for who we are still runs deep in the lives of many adults who often take decades, and sometimes a lifetime, to come to terms with the consequences of their lives and to find peace through acceptance of themselves.

If this were not a difficult enough task, consider the dilemma of the replacement child, one who is born to replace another child who has died, in its most basic definition. While many babies born after the death of another are welcomed into a family and loved for the unique individual they are, the replacement child carries the added burden of keeping their parent(s) focused on the forward motion of life in spite of unresolved grief which continues to haunt them, often for a lifetime. Barbara after Jeffrey. A mother's inability to see her daughter standing in her own light, out of the shadow of a brother she never knew.

The replacement child lives to please, lives to keep the peace, lives to be "good enough" in their parents' eyes. But the replacement child often falls short, not because of anything they've done, but because a parent who lives in grief also lives in the past—in the time before their child's death. The replacement child is supposed to be the "fixer," the one born to make up for the devastating loss but instead often ends up feeling like second best, the "replacement" for the original other, the one who was supposed to be here but isn't.

And then there are the limiting beliefs, the preconceived thoughts, ideas, and pronouncements seemingly written in stone, which are handed down from parent to child. Even questioning what is handed down to us as children often amounts to a kind of betrayal, for how can a child want anything different from a beloved parent who surely knows what's best for them?

When Will I Be Good Enough? A Replacement Child's Journey to Healing takes us on the twists and turns of a journey of self-discovery to a place of self-acceptance. It is a beautiful portrait of a life unfolding, blossoming into its full beauty. It is a story of taking control of one's life, of taking responsibility for becoming the person one is meant to be, of learning how to listen to one's own voice and of learning how to trust one's own internal compass. Barbara Jaffe teaches us that although we may never get the recognition we so deserve from those we want it most, we can ultimately get what we need from the best place imaginable—from within ourselves.

—Abigail Brenner, M.D.
Author of *Replacement Children: The Unconscious Script*
by Rita Battat Silberman & Abigail Brenner, M.D.

Prologue
The Beginning

It is good to have an end to journey towards; but it is the journey that matters in the end. —Ursula LeGuin

I am the replacement child—the child born after the tragic death of my brother whom I never knew—the almost two-year old cherub, whose giggling, dimpled, chubby face peers at me from multiple locations in antique frames strategically arranged throughout my childhood home. Jeffrey, the forever-perfect golden-hair little boy, who never had the opportunity to grow up and grow old. Jeffrey, whose place I suddenly took as "second" child, child Number Two. He was the family member about whom I wasn't supposed to talk or ask questions, yet through my mother's whispers and unspoken words, I implicitly knew I had to quite impossibly measure up to an unlived life.

"If Jeffrey had lived, you wouldn't have been born," my mother would often say throughout the years. Thus, even from an early age, I sensed that I must have done something horrific to cause my poor brother's demise. Such confusion solidified my mark as the little girl growing into young adulthood, the little girl who could and would do anything for the love of a mother whose heart was shattered into sharp pieces. I felt it my duty and my life's mission to pick up these jagged shards, one by one, and put them back together—in the form of my mother's broken heart. It took almost my entire life for me to realize that nothing I did could actually fix what was broken nor could I create my rightful place in a family whose blueprint had already been designed. I was and always would be 'second best'—second string—always on the bench waiting to be called, cheering from the bleachers, awaiting, in some way, my turn to be first—a turn that would never come.

I grew to recognize the variation between the mother I lived with and the one within the sepia edges of the black and white photos, scattered throughout our downstairs den. These pictorial revelations reflected my mother's pre-motherhood days, before loss replaced her inner glow with a grieving, wrinkled spirit. Her cascades of wavy, jet- black hair framed her olive-complexion. Such Romanesque beauty—defined by sculpted cheekbones and a strong, straight nose enhanced by her darkened lips, which in color became bright red, her signature shade. Her impeccably coordinated dresses and shoes revealed her slim, hourglass figure and shapely legs.

Yet, the mother I came to know spent most of her days lying in bed, sometimes for parts of a day, but always in bed each day.

My father would matter-of-factly comment, "Ma, she needs a lot of rest."

Yet, as a child, I was told that sick people stayed in bed. I intuitively knew, then, that my mother was ill, yet I could not hear her cough; I could not see her runny nose; nor was she doubled over with a stomachache. No, her ills were deep within, which no amount of supine positioning could restore. Over the years, I experienced my mother's withdrawal— always teetering on the edge of depression and exhaustion, yet still able to get through her daily life as if she were a leaf that falls from a tree, knowing its destination is the ground below but too fragile to land on target—always floating a little off the mark. Often, her bedroom door was closed, shut tightly like her heart, as if to seal herself from the pain that another child's love, and possible loss, could bring. For me, her daily long rests forever stamped within me the decision for my own life—to never lie in bed unless I literally could not step out of one. This was my fate, then; to dance as fast as I could without music; to keep busy when exhaustion took over; to will myself fine, when, at times, I was close to collapsing. Until today, I have never stayed in bed as long as I could walk and when I couldn't walk, I found a sofa—anything but a bed.

My parents, especially my mother, were encouraged by their respective parents and the old-time family doctor to have another child soon after their toddler died, so soon there was no time to formally and healthily grieve such a traumatic loss. How, then, can I truly understand such utter anguish and misery—the incomprehensible grief that enveloped my mother as she watched her baby lie dying in the hospital? How can I grasp my mother's traumatized shock and terror when this same family doctor, upon paying an evening house call, slapped her sharply across her face as a remedy for her uncontrolled wailing after burying her baby boy?

Following his facial blow, he simply added his verbal remedy, "You still have another child, so you have to move on. Have another."

So, how then can I truly realize her difficulty in moving

on when what she wanted to do was to melt into oblivion within her shade-drawn bedroom and her blankets?

Thus, I acknowledge that my mother's bedroom provided her a solace from the world that stole her baby boy, and a separation from the new life I represented. I do not blame my mother for what is lacking from my own core, but as a result of my permanent assignment as my dead brother's understudy, over the years, I have come to realize that parts of me were missing. I often felt like an empty pool in summer, forgotten-to-be-filled, awaiting completion, eerily vacant. While I have always sensed something has been 'off,' 'amiss,' 'lost,' 'separated,' for so long, I couldn't quite articulate this empty space within. However, as a result of growing up with a parent who was detached emotionally and loved conditionally, and at times fearfully, I have had to learn to reattach the threads from the left-over, mismatched tapestry of my soul. From the outside looking in, everything appears in place and complete. However, huge chunks were once vacant within me; I have learned to mold recreations of a healthy core based on the knowledge that something was amiss. I have, thus, spent a lifetime rebuilding myself from the inside out.

Today, I am intact, healthy, both physically and emotionally. At times I feel, actually, that I do not have a right to explore the components of my life that, in their entirety, view like a completed, well-developed film. An inner, old voice reminds me that others have life much worse, that they are homeless, physically limited, unloved, alone, yet I have come to a conclusion that all of us, whether complete or in the process, have had to deal with what can be deemed a "shadow-life"—a life that lives parallel within, reminding us all how far we have come, and must come, despite the challenges. To ignore our shadow-lives is to stop growing and learning—it is to lie in bed and wither, which I refuse to do.

For the most part, I live happily in a large life, with my energies and joys in so many areas of my personal and professional lives, yet I have worked for decades, non-stop, both through my own inner exploration and my formal academic education, to create my current inner and outer worlds.

This is not a book in which I place blame on my life's circumstances, which, quite frankly, today are joyful and positive. I merely examine the areas of my life, which as a young woman, I intuitively knew were 'off' and which ultimately limited so many of my decisions and choices as I grew into adulthood. When I was younger, I did not possess the understanding or experiences to articulate my missing, detached pieces, let alone begin to put myself back together. Now, though, I acknowledge that the slivers of my soul are intact and blended into a more intricate and more magnificent fabric than I could have ever imagined. I take ownership of my decisions that led me, at times, to both my searching for wholeness and my regression.

While this is my story, my journey, my awakenings, it can be anyone's—anyone who, with conviction, commits to reflection, introspection, and acknowledgment of one's shadow-life. It is my shadow-life, perhaps born from the seeds of the replacement child, yet I have learned to respectfully accept and nurture myself so that I might heal and continue to grow in unbelievably magnificent ways that I had not known possible.

I underscore the importance of the journey no matter where it begins or where it leads. To acknowledge my shadow life, embrace it and walk with it through the rest of my days is to give myself the respect, gratitude, and care that I deserve.

Chapter One
A Young Girl Slowly Disappearing

Any one of our human capacities, if unused out of fear or shame, leaves a small hole in the fabric of our self-esteem. —Gloria Steinem

We are all born with a survival instinct; of this I am sure. In my family of origin, my emotional existence depended on blending into our family's fabric that had already been woven. I morphed into the color beige without yet fully knowing that my vibrant soul screamed red, magenta, anything but blandness. And, thus, I learned to bury many of my desires, my thoughts, and my feelings at an early age. I became a passenger instead of a driver in my own life, ultimately taking the backseat in many of my decisions—deferring to almost anyone else whose opinion was stronger, mainly my mother's. I preferred for those around me to choose for me so I did not have the responsibility for negative outcomes—or any outcomes. As runner up, I got quite adept in my permanent role of second best. I became so proficient at feeling subtle nuances of others by taking the temperature of the room that I had long buried the barometer of my own life.

After my own birth, my mother was still recovering from Jeffrey's loss, so to get too attached too early, or at all, to another baby who also could die, was unimaginable. Thus, during my first year, my father got up nightly with me to give me my bottle, change my diaper, and calm me. In fact, as I grew into a toddler and little girl, when I had bad dreams, when I was sick, upset, or couldn't sleep, I called my father, knowing that to call my mother would have provoked the same response, "Barbara's calling," my mother would say, as she nudged my father awake, regardless of the fact that he would have to put in his usual 12-14 hours at the office the next day. Despite his exhaustion, he always lovingly came to me, hugging me against his protruding, round stomach and strong, smooth arms.

My young child's mind could not make sense of the existing confusion, for it was a time before language adequately detailed my developing emotions, yet a profound imprint took shape. Even when my understanding grew, I spent my early years ignoring what had been written indelibly upon my heart. While I ran into my father's arms to receive the unbridled cuddles and the warmth of his genuinely loving embrace, I encountered something far different when I ran to my mother. Even when her arms were open, they just could not envelope me with anticipatory joy. Rather with distance between her chest and my little-girl body of chubbiness and folds, she would look down at me as if examining a curious object.

After a few seconds, she would whisper with a slight push away from her body, "That's enough, Barbara" as if a timer had gone off within her reminding her to retract from the emotional discomfort of her child's hugs.

I have no doubt she loved me as her only daughter and youngest to my almost seven-year older brother. She worried about me constantly, and even as a little girl I understood that her extreme worry and her love were inexplicably blended.

"What's the matter?" she asked me quite often, with panic in her voice, as her eyes widened in fear. Especially if I suddenly turned quiet, which was so unlike my very talkative, little-girl self, she added. "Does anything hurt?" This question, as she looked deep into my eyes, often punctuated many of our conversations when she viewed me as off kilter. I was fine, almost always, and said as much, but she continued, "Are you sure? You have to tell me if anything hurts."

A poignant memory of my younger years, before I was completely independent in bathing, was when my mother washed my hair.

"Blondes use mayonnaise for conditioning, but we will use vinegar on your dark hair for shine."

It was the first time, and probably the only time, that I remember feeling relieved that I was a brunette. It was not the washing of my hair that provided me with such joy, for the vinegar stank and burned, but when she dried my hair, I was in heaven. She sat on the toilet seat cover and I kneeled next to her with my head resting on her thighs. The towel was around my head as she dried it slowly. I never wanted it to end. No words were usually spoken, but in those moments, I knew that she was completely mine and even my older brother Stephen did not have this experience. Towel drying was one of my highlights in my young life. I wanted her to continue this ritual, but when I was old enough to take showers, she deemed it over.

"You can wash and dry your own hair now."

I was well taken care of. Mother cared for me physically and made sure I stayed healthy. She gave me the toys I yearned for and those I had begged for, often advertised on television. Clothes, shoes, and everything else were brought home to me before I needed them and when I wanted them. If there was a new cereal that I was desperate to try, especially one with a toy inside the box, I had only to mention the name and it was on her next market list. I grew into a young girl who didn't question my parents' love or devotion—both my mother's and my father's. Yet, as such a young child, I also did not have the necessary means to examine the dynamics that were established soon after I became a walking, talking person for unlike my father, my mother came to me, to most of our interactions, with a heaviness that I could not interpret.

By the age of seven, though, I had assumed my role. My goal, then, before I knew why, was to make my mother happy, to make her smile, and to make her love me more than anyone else in the entire world. My soul cried out: *Look at me! Tell me what to do and I'll do it, Mommy!* I wanted to snap my fingers and make her come alive, giving her the jolt of energy she needed to focus on my inner world—one that needed no clothes or shoes but complete attention. Little could I know at the young age of ten that nothing I could ever do, say or be would change her eternally grieving soul. When I was conceived so soon after Jeffrey's death, she was not ready for me. In fact, she was never going to be ready for me.

Nothing stopped my desire for her attention, though. My perennial optimism forced me into a funny little girl making silly comments as I impersonated singers, dancers, and anyone whom my mother appreciated. I memorized lyrics to Broadway show tunes and sang them for her upon command; I copied the actions of TV personalities and in my mother's bedroom, right in front of her bed, I jumped and bounced on the beige plush carpet and performed, while she lay in her king-sized bed, supported by her cadres of pillows propping her up, always with the television on low volume right to the side of my performances.

My mother's attention, though, was fleeting and each new scene or vignette was short lived, punctuated by her definitive comment, "That's nice, Barbara, now that's enough."

Even then, I knew I could not compete, as Stephen's natural comedic talents completely overshadowed anything I could do and truly I was second best to them both—a dead brother and my older living brother. Stephen, dark-haired, olive complexion and slim, who looked much more like my mother than my father, was genuinely funny and I just wasn't, despite trying so hard. He could contort his face into Jerry Lewis-like expressions that made my mother so hysterical that she belted out the laugh we all loved most—that deep, deep belly roar that contagiously made us naturally join her in her joyful frenzy of delight. I was to be laughed at because I was cute, but my pixie haircut, glistening black eyes and impish smile could not overshadow my expanding roundness, which my mother addressed immediately.

Through my mother's eyes, she saw her chubby daughter growing into a heavy teenager. To my father, I was just fine, perhaps because he was plump, himself. He loved to eat and expected everyone around him to feel and do the same. He lived for his meals and believed that life was to be experienced through chewing and swallowing the very best life had to offer at every meal. When my father saw that I was hesitant in eating something he knew I usually enjoyed, he always remarked:

"Nothing wrong with you, Barbara. Eat!"

I grew to ignore my father's words, for my mother's comments always superseded his. I learned to watch everything I ate—at all times. I became adept at the process of inspecting my food, its caloric intake, and my mother's silent responses and her oh-so-quick glances at my plate. Every meal we shared became a game of inner control with outward rewards and self-punishment.

Fear over the depth of my chubbiness was reinforced during my pediatrician visits, simply because of the scale. My ancient pediatrician, Dr. Boast, with his straightforward, no-nonsense way with words, must have corroborated with my mother before one of my official annual weigh-ins. The mere thought of entering the sterile, antiquated exam room and approaching the upright, rickety metal scale actually made me panic, a scenario practiced in my mind days before the big visit. I pleaded for the first appointment of the day so that I could stand on the scale with an empty stomach. While I didn't want to show my nakedness to not only the doctor, but to my mother, who always accompanied me into the exam room, at least I could remove some additional ounces if I completely disrobed. Either way, I lost.

After I walked off the scale, he uttered one short sentence that would forever reverberate within my mind, long past my earlier years:

"With your body-type, you would have survived the Holocaust."

As a young girl, of course, I had no understanding of what was meant by this comparative reference to the most horrific documented genocide of the 20th century. He followed up this ridiculous non-sequitur with his explanation of what he figured was my slow metabolism, finally getting to his point—that I didn't need much food to get through the day, thus the reference to a possible death-camp survival. Apparently, with my bulky build, he thought I would have endured daily starvation. Of course, his additional comment to my mother, within my range of hearing, about signing me up for a football team as a linebacker due to my broad shoulders, just reinforced my decision to pursue my withering away process.

"And, with those wide hips, Barbara, you won't have any problems having babies one day."

I was horrified and speechless to respond to his reference to the female part of me related to the birthing process, so far away from my little girl mind that still desired my own status as our family's baby. In a few short minutes, Dr. Boast had reduced to me to football shoulders, birthing hips, and a keen ability to starve.

All of the planning and ruminating about the scale, which became larger than life, really added up to a version of his usual comments:

"You're 'up' from last year, Barbara...five pounds. Do you know what will happen if you continue to gain five pounds each year?"

Again, I returned to a stomach full of nothingness at an age when I was still playing with my baby dolls. My internalized message, established by the time I was twelve, then, was quite loud and clear—my self-worth, and as a result, my self-esteem, were deeply connected to the numbers indicated on our family's scale; in my doctor's annual charts; and within my mother's field of vision.

By 14, then, I became an expert at watching my mother as I ate, checking her expression for signals of approval, or even worse, disapproval, so after a while, she didn't even have to articulate her thoughts. Before I knew what an eating disorder was, before such topics became a mainstream understanding with gentle psychological support and therapeutic programs, especially for young girls, I had entered the mystifying world of anorexia. The disease grew slowly, but when I got results in the form of positive comments about my melting pounds, I upped my lack-of-eating strategy. I began to experiment with fewer calories, with more exercise, with even more secrets. I learned that I could bite into my sandwich, store the pieces in my mouth, excuse myself from my family's dining table, go into my bedroom and spit out the chewed up bread and cheese. I wadded the food into a ball and buried it in a napkin at the bottom of my trashcan. No one ever found out. Of course, I feared that I had probably swallowed some of the sandwich, so I immediately got down on the floor and completed about 50 sit-ups and push-ups to rid myself of the estimated additional five calories.

After my regime of eating but not really eating, and the bedroom floor exercises, I examined myself in the full-length mirror attached to the inside of my closet door. Sideways, front and back, with a hand-held mirror so I could see my backside. Puffy parts meant a continued day's deprivation, but if they were flat and I could see a hipbone or a rib, then all was well with my secret little world of deprivation.

I did not understand the compulsion that possessed me in the form of a classic eating disorder. I only knew that when my parents—especially my mother—told me to eat, I ate less. Many of our dinners became battlefields, with almost the same monologue by my mother:

"Eat, Barbara. You like meatloaf. You always ate baked potatoes."

"Just put it on your fork and put it in your mouth."

"I've had it. Enough is enough. I can't keep this up. Do you know what you're doing to me?"

Soon, I refused to eat much at all until my periods stopped; until I frequently fainted; and until my mother, in her frantic concern, brought me to her doctor. Such compassionate wisdom from her female gynecologist was to remind me how much I was hurting my mother as a result of my self-starvation.

"You know, Barbara, when you don't eat, you're upsetting your mother," counseled Dr. Chin.

I was secretly happy to have both my mother's attention and the familiar hunger pains that defined my days and flattened my stomach. My starvation recovery was nightly physical therapy, designed by my mother yet implemented by both of my parents. I was told to sit on my twin bed, and in front of me, they placed a plate of eight Oreo cookies and a glass of milk. Both she and my father watched me slowly ingest what normally could have been a non-nutritious yet delicious childhood treat, with my mom's evening mantra:

"I can't take this anymore. You'd better stop this and start eating. We're going to keep doing this every night until you stop it and wake up." And, always, she ended her frantic, powerlessness by, "You know, you're killing Daddy and I."

After they watched me swallow each Oreo and drink the milk, I was made to stand on the scale, which, in a very serious action, had been carried in from the bathroom and placed on my bedroom shag carpet. The guilt I felt in hurting my mother as a result of my starvation even superseded my desire to starve myself, so I did as I was told and ate each cookie brought forth. Actually, though, I did learn a valuable lesson in those early years of denial. I learned to eat around my mother, minimally, but at least eat. I just starved myself during other parts of the day; strategically and calculatingly, I saved my daily food intake to eat in front of her and all was well. The only result of my Oreo-cookie recovery from my anorexia was the fact that I have never eaten another Oreo cookie since. My food issues were always complicated, for my mother reminded me when I plumped up again after my three years of starvation. All she had to say was, "I think you should watch it," and I was sent immediately back to my pre-Oreo deprivation.

When I was skin and bones, she enticed me with new clothes only if I were to gain back some weight.

"I'll buy you whatever you want. It will be my greatest pleasure. Just eat," she both pleaded and commanded.

I did gain weight but not for the prize of new additions to my closet. I was given the go-ahead to eat, so I went to the other extreme. Basically, I began to eat again just because I loved food; I loved food more than clothing, but because my mother acknowledged my thinness, I ran with her approval. I had an amazing appetite and could eat complete pizzas long before individual-sized portions were available. I desired meat—steaks, prime rib, beef ribs, anything dense and richly satisfying, yet I did not crave sweets. I just loved anything I could chew—the bigger the chunks, the better, all adding the pounds erased in my skeletal days. I comforted myself with the food I had deprived myself of for so many months. Once again, I was chunky. Consequently, nothing I wore fit well, reinforced by our painful twosome shopping trips back to the 'Chubbette' clothing line.

"You look much better now," yet I perceived Mom didn't really mean her carefully chosen words.

The styles of the late 60s and early 70s, hot-pants, mini-skirts and go-go boots, and tightly ribbed t-shirts, took in no account for my pubescent roundness and curves. Especially problematic were pants, but if we found a pair that actually fit my small waist, big hips, and even bigger thighs, Mom announced, "We will buy one in every color." And so we did.

Searching for clothes that fit and still looked 'cool' for a young self-conscious teen of the Flower Power generation was like going into battle—one I often lost. Mostly, I found adorable, perfect pants, shirts, and dresses that were unsuitable for my adolescent, very full, hour-glass figure. Clothing that did fit was quite hideous and belonged in another department, certainly not the young, trendy girl's section. However, when a shirt fit or even the almost impossible pair of pants, my mother's most important edict was that nothing could be too tight, especially around the bottom or the bust line; in fact, the looser the better.

I got great at the dressing room calisthenics my mother taught me—the clothing exercises that tested the 'give' of the material. She got up from the bench inside the fitting room, and gave me the seat.

"Sit down and see if the pants sit with you," she would command and would then add, "Stretch your arms behind your back and if the buttons move, the shirt is too tight."

My mother's adage was always, "If in doubt, one size up." Unless it were my school gym clothes—then several sizes up. I did what she asked, contorting my body that was enveloped by the new clothing. How could I not? It was the only way to end the shopping spree and as much as I wanted to go home, I wanted clothing even more. My mother's ways to measure whether my clothing fit eventually morphed into my own as I grew, relieved that there were no hidden cameras behind these doors.

When I began 7th grade, we purchased the regulation physical education clothing, referred to as 'bloomers.' The bright blue, all-in-one, short jumpsuit with elastic around the waist and the thighs likened a chunky person, such as myself, to a sack of potatoes. Nothing about the 100% cotton 'garbage-bag-like' construction was flattering for any female larger than a size 5. In those days, I was probably smaller than I thought, but not in my gym clothes. In fact, this unflattering 7th grade uniform was the exact same one, with frequent washings, worn through 12th grade in high school, lasting six full academic years. It wasn't that I didn't grow in those years; it was just that I had finally grown into my uniform. My mom had created one of the first one-size-fits-all physical education garbs, yet I was the only buyer.

Despite the difficulty in shopping for every-day clothes to conceal my folds, when bathing suit season came upon me, there was just no hiding or justice. During these times, my mother employed the big guns—Nana Bea. My loving, 5'1", silver-haired, maternal grandmother was commanded to accompany us to multiple locations until we actually captured swimsuits, or, as was always the case, one swimsuit in multiple colors. Nana Bea was the only female in my family who understood me. It was as if she and I were cut from the same cloth. She never said anything about the pounds I carried, and while no one talked about eating disorders, my mother shared with me that Nana had tried countless diets in her day and even starved herself and fainted. She was always weight conscious and carried her full hourglass figure quite eloquently despite her diminutive height. She was probably much like me—a budding anorexic, so I think she understood the angst of my chubbiness in a sea of skinniness. Bikinis were completely out of the question; every part of me was round. Two-pieced bathing suits were the only choice, as, in those days, all-in-one swimsuits solely existed for old women whose thighs were even bulkier than mine, and those on a swim team.

I was plump and very vain, so there was no way I was going to wear an all-in-one old lady's swimsuit at the age of 15 despite my mother's pleas:

"It doesn't matter how you look in the pool. No one will see you. Just get what is flattering. What do you care?"

Oh, but I did. I cared so much. After my fits in the dressing rooms in multiple stores and her yelling she "was done," a gallant search by both my mother and my grandmother produced at least one semi-acceptable two-piece with a skirt to cover the top of my dimply thighs and one that expanded over my wide bottom. My mother clapped in victory, slapping her hand against her leg as she did with great, unforeseen accomplishments. Soft-spoken Nana Bea was satisfied, actually more relieved, that her duty was completed, weathering my short-lived tears, yet she felt the need to finalize the deal:

"You really do look fine in the suit, Barbara. I wouldn't steer you wrong."

But, already my talents lay in reading between the lines, so I interpreted her words differently: "It's the best you're going to do under the circumstances. Maybe next bathing suit season, you'll look different and you'll have more to choose from. At least this year's fiasco is over."

I, too, knew deep down that this suit was not appealing or flattering. How could the two-piece garb be attractive in a bright, solid color with so much material? I looked like a giant piece of yellow fruit, a round casaba. Minutes of arguing, hours of crying, and days of searching all culminated in the polyester neon yellow two-piece with a built in rubbery bra—in two other equally disastrous colors. They weren't pretty, cute, trendy, or very feminine. Then again, I was chubby, so I had limitations, always exaggerated in June, July, and August. My only hope was to spend the majority of my swimming time submerged in the water and strategically place a towel near the edge of the pool so no one would see me waddle up the dreaded three-step ladder.

With all the traditionally normal confusion and craziness within the head of a female adolescent budding into young womanhood, I fed off of my mother's frequent comments about some of my skinny friends or even emaciated television actresses.

"She is so tiny, so thin, and so cute!"

Her remarks reminded me that while she certainly didn't want me to starve, I had to stay vigilant, always on top of whittling away extra poundage. I was becoming more linguistically competent at interpreting language with every glazed donut I inhaled; thus, I had my own translation of my mother's seemingly innocuous words. What I heard was, "She is so tiny, so thin, and *therefore*, so cute." One little change from 'and' to 'therefore' solidified my lifetime battle with the permanent connection between beauty and thinness. They were inextricable; they became one; and they, in turn, sadly formed my unviable goal of a size, weight, and shape that was impossible for anyone to attain, let alone my big-boned frame. However, my determination to at least try to become skinny, slim, slender, sleek, created a life-long, familiar and comforting experience of deprivation.

Socially, I was never really fat enough to be ostracized like some unfortunate young girls and I was just pleasant-looking enough not to be labeled in teenage language as a dork, today's geek or nerd. I had friends and best friends, and even boyfriends, young boys who were attracted to my outgoing personality, pleasant face and perhaps even the clever ways I hid my pounds. I envied the type of best friends who decided on the phone, late at night, what to wear to school the next day and then exchange clothing in the girl's bathroom. I knew I certainly couldn't exchange my size for anyone's. Yet, I had my best friends, real pals, who, despite our closeness, also never knew the internal suffering I was enduring—Lori and Michelle.

Lori, a freckled-face, brunette, with a beanpole figure, never worried about what entered her mouth, but equally never viewed me as someone who needed to either. Weight was never her frame of reference, and I loved her for that. Like mine, her family adored food, and they ate when they wanted and what they wanted. If they felt like Chinese food at midnight, they would drive to San Francisco's Chinatown without even thinking about the next day's consequences for calories and limitations. Oh, how I adored her dear family and their freedom from obsessive thoughts of calories and chubbiness.

Michelle was my height, about 5'5" with an olive-complexion like mine. Her silky long black hair covered plump shoulders. She was mostly a little heavier than I, but like Lori, she was never preoccupied about what she ate and her family, too, encouraged enjoyment of food without limitations. When I was at her house, which was almost daily, her mother encouraged me to eat the baklava that always rested on their white-tile kitchen counter.

"One, please," yet I never shared with Michelle my internal torture of licking the last bite of honey and pistachios off of my fingers, knowing of the next day's dire consequences. I adored being with them both and was amazed that Lori ate whatever she wanted without gaining an ounce and Michelle ate whatever she wanted without caring if she did gain. While I was in the middle of the continuum between these two little girls, my goal was clear. I desired to look like skinny Lori, and savor my food without caring like easy-going Michelle.

Perhaps like other young females across the country at that time, I went through a period when I would mesmerizingly watch Miss Teenage America on television and dreamily hope to try out for the title. At the same time, I contemplated trying out for our junior high school's cheerleaders, but I wasn't oblivious to the fact that all of these girls—both the Teenage Americas and the cheerleaders—were skinny with stick-like extremities. My plumpness was evenly spread out—arms, legs, thighs. I asked my mother the loaded question, already knowing the answer.

"Do you think I could ever make it to a pageant?"

I appreciated her honesty about whether I had a shot at either—the pageants or the cheers, for she reinforced my own thoughts that my thighs were just too thick. In fairness to her, she never articulated the word 'no,' but she shook her head, indicating that these dreams would always be thus. My voracious appetite and thick thighs squelched my dream of cheers and national adventures.

No matter what I looked like below my neck, I was told countless times that I had a pretty face. When I was with my mother and we would run into one of her friends or acquaintances, the woman would smile at me yet direct her seemingly flattering words to my mom, "Your daughter has such a pretty face." It took me a while to finally understand my strange, unsettling feeling resulting from what I initially interpreted as kind words. The words were positive, but when I processed the semantics, I understood the real meaning: *Your daughter would be pretty all over if she weren't fat.* The light bulb went off and I understood, indeed. The words implied that my face was a separate entity, or at least should have been.

Such comments further helped me to learn to read in between the lines. I interpreted another two-sided compliment quite adeptly: "You have lost so much weight." These words were especially hard-hitting when I hadn't actually lost anything.

"This is the thinnest you have ever been," was uttered when I was twenty pounds overweight. But, the worst of all, was a simple yet piercing remark from my mother: "You should watch it." Those four words threw me into a tailspin with the now-effortless translation, "You are getting fat again."

By 16, I was over my complete starvation days, yet I was quite adept at returning to the familiar and strangely comforting hunger pains that I learned to accept as positive reinforcement, especially during times of stress and sadness. My mother's words signaled a pattern almost imprinted within my DNA; I ate a lot and then starved a lot. All it took was such a comment to reinforce my skipping breakfast and lunch while eating a small dinner. I could comfortably survive on a starvation diet, for I found odd consolation in personal denial simultaneously accompanied by my mother's anxious attention.

My older brother Steve was relieved of my mother's eagle eye; apparently his gender and his birth order saved him in this way. Steve was freer to be himself and freer to eat what he wanted, and did so without guilt or apologies or my mother's stares. He appeared to have a normal relationship with food and indulged to satiation with delight as I longingly and emptily watched with a sense of injustice. Often after he returned home from high school, he took out an entire Sara Lee pound cake and proceeded to eat most, if not all, as a snack. How I envied his ability to down an entire cake while not even thinking about the repercussions of calories and weight gain or, most of all, our mother's reproach.

My eating disorder was not the fault of my mother, for she most likely was trying to make my future easier; my childhood and teenage years, especially, were a time in our culture where pencil-thin females were the sign of beauty; anorexia hadn't been formally mentioned or described as its rightful moniker as a psychological disorder. It was a time before the issue of female body acceptance was front-page material. However, in my role as the replacement child, the child who felt she had no room for imperfections, physical or emotional, I became the ideal breeding ground for my eating issues. I controlled the only element of my life that my mother couldn't—my food intake. It became my silent battle of destruction, from within, with no winner. My mother's only daughter, child number three, who was really number two, a needed-to-be-seen young girl, required attention, whether fat or thin.

The seed of my eating disorder—the foundation of my weight-fate, was cultivated and enhanced by a crazy old-time pediatrician and a nervous, worried-about-what-people-thought mother. She was determined to keep her daughter alive, yet at the same time, not fat and pretty, two diametrically opposed qualities in Her Book, filled with rules to live by and slogans for me to internalize.

Chapter Two
My Mother's Book:
Mandates and Mantras

It's never too late—in fiction or in life—to revise.
—Nancy Thayer

While my eating issues continued to define our relationship, my mother regularly educated me from Her Book, denoting her own version of life lessons—an orally-communicated doctrine, shared with me from childhood and throughout our lives together, whether person-to-person or on the phone. I intuitively knew that while there was no written manual, my daily lessons required taking pages from her oral text and memorizing the lessons and sayings. In referencing her self-acclaimed sage advice, my mother began many of her sentences with, "In my book…" which was really all I needed to hear before she told me what she thought I should do in most every facet of my life. Just as in school, I was a dutiful student and soon learned information necessary to live a subservient, people-pleasing life—all compiled from my mother's version of her own Bible.

Besides educating me on food, she always reminded me about what to wear; how to wear it; how to accessorize jewelry; how to nurture friendships; how to treat a mother (one of her favorite topics); and, most important, how to defer to her through my loyalty, excluding others, even my father, emphasized by her consistently spoken mantra, "You only have one mother."

While I could have responded with an in-kind comment, "You only have one daughter," this would have been cruel because as the replacement child, my existence was tenuous, at best. Plus, if we were to have a conversation in which I shared my thoughts and feelings, she would respond with, "Don't be fresh," her code for any response that was contrary to hers. "Don't be fresh" meant, *Don't upset me and don't share your feelings.* If I continued to voice my opinion, she went on to the next level of response, much more deadly, *Don't cross me!* Hearing these three words prepared me for what was to come—I would pay for my retorts for hours and sometimes days, in her silence, as she closed her bedroom door to me. I, who loved books, anything with writing, anything related to communication, was emotionally isolated with no words, a painful detachment from the woman I adored.

My mother recognized my love of school and my unstoppable academic work ethic and at the same time, she wanted to prepare me for the disappointments I would encounter even at such a young age. Long before I understood metaphors, she introduced me to one of her mantras: *It's better to be middle of the road.* In elementary school, IQ tests were given to determine how smart we all were. From those tests, and for all six subsequent years—tracking occurred, where students were put together into classes or taken out of their classes for special programs. On the first day of third grade, I came home crying because my best friend Lori and some other kids were taken out of our class and would be each day for 'special' work, of which I wouldn't be a part. My mother called the principal to ask if I could join this selected group, especially to be with Lori, but her request was denied. In framing her 'talk' to me, my mother pulled out an official letter from her closet, the sacred space where she kept her jewelry, money, special papers, and hidden candy. The important document was filled with numbers, numbers that made no sense to an eight-year old, but she summarized the only real important part.

"Remember the test you took last year? You know you aren't a good test taker. Anyway, it's better to be middle of the road, fewer problems that way. When people are really smart, there is a fine line...."

My little girl head couldn't capture the non-sequitur phrases nor could I fill in the blanks of her entire explanation. As Mother kept talking, I only focused on what was to be repeated so often throughout my earlier educational years, another one of her adages: *It's better to be middle of the road.* I didn't know exactly what these words meant then, but I soon came to understand the only important results of the test.

I wasn't accepted into the gifted group, Lori's group, because I wasn't gifted. Borderline, maybe, but I didn't quite make the cut. I was, just as my mother said, *middle of the road*, which was apparently more than acceptable in my mother's book but never in mine. Throughout school, Mother reminded me often of these words, when I had a difficult test to study for, or when I decided to take a challenging class. By 6th grade, I was accepted into the special "Gifted Program," but it felt gratuitous, a consolation prize, and besides, by then, I felt as if I were *middle of the road.*

As I grew, this slogan forever created a standard for which I refused to meet, yet the price I paid for vigilant excellence was immeasurable. Her simple phrase haunted me even when I received A's on exams in most of my courses, way beyond my elementary years. My years of education were colored by my mother's phrase that attempted to classify, define, and limit my academic potential into the dreaded "average" category. Even when I earned top scores on papers and exams, a little voice within my own head reminded me that the competitive grades had to be mistakes; perhaps I was just lucky. I couldn't quite comprehend how I managed a 4.0 when I was forever average. Nowhere did I connect my grades with my intelligence.

My grades, and my consistently strong academic performance were forever the universe's sense of humor, showing that even a student of basic intelligence could excel through persistence. My mother confirmed this internal dialogue often by adding, "You've always been a hard worker," which would have been a compliment if she hadn't also included the reminder that I had also always "worked up to my potential." I astutely read between the lines—brilliant people didn't have potential to work up to—they were just intelligent, plain and simple. While Mother did not add the word 'limited' before the word 'potential,' she didn't have to, for that was my job, which, sadly, I did quite well for many years.

My mother's Book was also filled with slogans based on her life philosophy and as a young girl, I internalized these phrases as part of my own language, long before I knew their subliminal messages. *I'm only here in case of fire* addressed her own frustrations. Basically, when she felt unappreciated by all of us, and life, she spoke about fires. Apparently, she felt taken advantage of; overworked in the house; barely valued. Like a dutiful daughter, I often responded with the only comment that made sense to me and one that would attempt to make her feel better.

"That's not true, Mom; I need you all the time," which wasn't far from the truth.

Mother responded with virtually the same emphatic words each time, "No, you don't. You really don't."

And so it was, almost the same verbal exchange between us every time she reminded me that she was virtually superfluous in her role as mother, except for her role as protector against flames.

This quite ridiculous statement was also interestingly ironic. I was a three-year old playing with my toys on the living room floor when a large San Francisco earthquake struck; my mother literally ran out of the house leaving me alone. When her friend Joyce ran out with her, it was Joyce who panicked, and ran back into the house, yelling, "You forgot Barbara. She's still in the house." This family lore was one about which we all laughed when Joyce would repeat it almost every time I saw her over the years. "I saved you," she reminded me. Apparently, my mother literally meant what she said, that she really was only there in case of fire, just not earthquakes.

Perhaps it was not a surprise that Mother's adage focused on fires and not earthquakes, as she was definitely Missing in Action with regards to tremblers, yet this did not stop her from protecting her own mother, while attempting to sacrifice her own daughter. During a family vacation in Palm Springs when I was 11, my parents and I were in our motel room when a large, rolling earthquake began.

My mother yelled to me: "Go get Nana!"

My grandmother was in another room far on the other side of the pool.

"Barbara shouldn't leave the room, Marge," my concerned father added, but his opinions never mattered much, especially when his mother-in-law could be in danger.

Who better to send 'out there' during a natural disaster than the one expendable, obedient, people-pleaser? I opened the door to our room and literally ran with the motion of the trembler. I felt alive with a mission—saving my grandmother and following my mother's orders, never once thinking about my own safety or the fact that I should not have been asked to be my grandmother's savior at an age when I still needed my own protection.

The quake seemed to continue for quite a while, yet, of course, it probably lasted no longer than 15 seconds. Being careful not to trip, I was running parallel to the pool, whose water was sloshing out everywhere. I ran with the rhythmic movements of the earth until I got to my grandmother's room.

"You shouldn't have come. I'm fine, but you could've been hurt," was what my concerned Nana lovingly said to me.

When my grandmother asked her own daughter why I was the appointed emissary sent to save her, my mother only responded, "I was worried about you being alone, Mom."

The saddest element of this recount, of course, was that after my mother's directive and even during the event, I never once questioned my own safety; at that age, the need to please my mother superseded even my own survival instinct.

I did my best to limit her use of the fire motif by deferring to her as much as possible. Often, the demonstration of her affection for me was based on whether I agreed to wear what she placed, nightly, on the unused twin bed next to my own. If I defiantly fought her on her clothes selection, she would often utter another one of her infamous phrases, "*I don't know what I did to deserve this,*" and I was forever left to interpret the meaning of 'this.' The definition wasn't as important as my resulting guilt. Her 'deserving' remarks became her overall catch phrase, used throughout my life, depending on what I said and did.

"I hate that plaid dress, Mom. It makes me look fat."

She responded with her usual comment when I spoke about such things:

"You liked it when I bought it, so you'll wear it. It doesn't make you look any heavier than anything else you have and besides, nice girls wear dresses on photo day. That's enough, Barbara. *I don't know what I did to deserve this.*"

When she felt terribly frustrated, emotionally overworked, and put-upon by anyone and everyone, when she wasn't talking about fires, another catch phrase surfaced: *Peace at any price.* These words never referred to the need to keep our home peaceful despite the difficulty of life. Mother's adage was a paradox of sorts, for I understood that there would be no peace when she uttered this phrase. The real definition of the adage was about swallowing her anger; her frustrations; her resentments, often at family members—parents, uncles and aunts, mostly on my father's side of the family. Her bedroom door slammed; pots found a cracking drumbeat against the kitchen tiles. Phone receivers banged, all with her message to stay clear.

I learned, then, that her phrase had little to do with peace; the price paid was to witness my mother's withdrawal and detachment when she became so upset at swallowing her own frustrations at her relatives or life. My mother's *peace at any price* ironically resulted in the loss of my own peace and my serenity, for at these times, she detached farther from me, and all of us because she was so upset dealing with the conflict within.

"Once again, I'm the only one to have holiday dinners. I have to worry about Daddy's family, my own family, and everyone else. If I don't have them over, they will have no place to go. It's enough. I really can't take it."

My mother was always conflicted, for she wanted to take care of her own family—her mother, her aunts, her brother and his wife and children, yet she also felt a dutiful obligation, mixed with love, for my father's side of the family, who had no one else who cared as much as my own parents. My mother always knew the right thing to do in these situations and she created bountiful and delicious spreads at every holiday for at least 20-30 people. She entertained beautifully but not before having been spent with her tirades of planning and frustration, followed by a few days after the events of lying in bed to regain her strength, all due to her *peace at any price* mandate.

It was an on-the-job lesson of learning how to swallow my feelings and defer to another's. While I watched my mother do this in her own relationships with our family members, I learned quite well to squelch whatever I felt. Soon I, too, uttered the phrase even before I knew the results of such a meaningless, pointless, and quite self-destructive phrase to live by.

Peace between us often depended on how I acted and responded to, not just my choice of clothing, but my interactions with "the aunties"—my great aunts, my grandmother's sisters. There were four of them—all forces to be reckoned with; they were a collective unit and came together as such at parties, at family affairs, even on the phone. In engaging with them, my mother always reminded me to *bow to age*, her version of 'showing respect' for anyone older than I, who actually was everyone in our family. I learned this lesson of deference from my mother's Book very well. If I voiced my own opinions or feelings to my grandmother, contrary to hers, my mother, not my grandmother, would reference her ditty on age which often accompanied a monologue on disrespect, which my mother referred to as fresh.

Sometimes I just didn't want to be with my beloved grandmother, so when she started up a conversation, I responded as the frustrated preteen that I was:

"Nana, I really don't feel like talking to you now. I'm sorry. I don't want to tell you about my day. It was a day like all of them. I just got home from school and I have tons of homework."

My mother's eyebrows immediately raised and I knew I had crossed the line into 'freshness,' reminding me to bow to age.

"That was fresh. Sure, it's fine for Nana to make your snack and do what you need. She was only asking about your day."

The slogan, though, was mostly utilized by my mother when I wanted something though not understanding why the answer had to be 'no'. Perhaps it was a seemingly more

considerate version of "Because I said so." There was no arguing;
I was not permitted to voice my opinions and feelings. Such a
phrase only referred to my communication between generations,
of which there were two above me and none below. In my
frustrations with my grandmother at times, my mother would
only say, "*Bow to age.*" Case closed. I learned to bow even when I
didn't need to; I learned to bow even when age was not involved.
I learned, thus, to bow to most everyone's desires but my own.
I followed the rules, yet within me was a rebellious side not far
beneath the surface reminding me that something didn't quite
fit, that I didn't quite fit.

Perhaps it was the genetics I inherited from my father,
whose personality was much closer to my own. He was a
sweet, easy-going, loving and supportive man, whose main
flaw was his hopeless devotion to his wife, deferring to her
for everything, and reminding me that, "Your mother is the
captain of the ship at home and I am the captain of the ship
at the office," a mantra repeated so often, I actually created a
nautical vision of my parents.

I was immediately deflated by the lack of any support
I could obtain from my demonstrative father, except to know
that he loved me unconditionally; yes, I knew that for sure. My
mother sensed my strong attachment and connection to my
father and when she was extremely frustrated over my lack of
acquiescence to her requests, she would yell, "You think your
father is so nice? Well, he's not so easy to live with. I could tell
you stories…"

The jealousy behind her words was an emotion foreign to
me, so I didn't quite comprehend the impact of her statement.

Perhaps Mother intuitively understood that I preferred to be with the parent who looked at me as if I could do no wrong. Actually, my mother's chapter on motherly love excluded fatherly love. Absolute loyalty belonged to her and my father was too busy at work to really care, reinforced by his frequent mandate, "Do what your mother says. She is always right." And, he meant it along with a perceived relief in not having to deal with a prepubescent female.

No matter how often I referenced Mother's chapter on clothing, this topic became a major control issue between us. While she couldn't completely stop me from eating or not eating, she could decide what I could buy and what I couldn't. Nothing was more prevailing than my obsessive desire to own a pair of jeans, but in my Mother's Book, uniqueness meant that I could not look like everyone else. I screamed:

"But I want jeans! I need them! Everyone has a pair. I'm the only one who doesn't and I look like a dork in my regular pants."

Mom responded with her final words on the subject:

"Absolutely not. No jeans! They're common, ordinary. Just because everyone wears them doesn't mean you have to. You're better than that. They do nothing for you and you don't need to look like everyone else."

Actually, as a teenager, I wanted to blend in; I wanted to own a pair of Levis even if it meant I would look like everyone else. It was the 60s in San Francisco—the Hippie Movement, free love, Golden Gate Park, flower power, and all I wanted was to wear a pair of dark blue Levis. But, I could not—all through junior high and high school, I never owned one pair. I literally had to wait to purchase the jeans until after I graduated from high school and went away to college.

As I became old enough to venture outside the house without my mother, she stressed that it was better to be out with a girlfriend who I didn't like than spend my time alone in the house, especially on the weekends. She reminded me of how important it was to be 'seen'—to be out and about socially regardless of the fact that she, herself, chose to lay in bed most days.

"You never know who you will run into or your friend might know someone—a friend of a friend."

I didn't like the thought of spending time with friends like Jane, who was phony and limited in her conversations, yet well-connected and social, so initially, I followed her friendship mandates. My Saturdays were filled like an old-fashioned dance card; I made sure to make plans with a friend or acquaintance, most any female, even if my companion wasn't someone I really enjoyed. This ridiculous acceptance of spending time with girls with whom I had few shared interests and who I didn't enjoy, lasted far too long until I decided I would rather stay home, alone in my bedroom, than to have empty conversations. I sacrificed my mother's approval of my social life in order to stop the charade of pretending I had mutual interests with girls who also cared more about who they would see at our lunches and it wasn't me. My mother merely emphasized that in her book popular girls were always out there. Clearly, I wasn't defined as popular.

Ironically, though, as I got older, a profound effect of my less-than-pleasant get-togethers was the flip side of the coin—I was included, which admittedly felt quite positive. I was included in parties and lunches, get-togethers, and sleepovers.

Invitations came from a variety of girls because I was seen, as my mother stated. While I didn't enjoy these events any more than the one-on-one lunches with girls with whom I had little in common, I took away an underlying feeling that has sadly accompanied me my entire life. The feeling of being included was so profound that I soon needed to be part of a group of females about whom I didn't really care. When I was not invited, it was of little consequence that I did not want to be at the event. I still irrationally wanted to be included.

I viewed the direct connection between my inclusion on the guest list and my self-worth. If I was invited, then I was worthy and if I was overlooked, I was not. How amusing that I wanted to be invited to a party to which I didn't want to attend. How pathetic. I lived with this irrational feeling and had to come to terms with this paradox so that I could put the pieces back to a whole life. It was the basic act of inclusion, nothing more—the legacy of a replacement child who knew she wasn't on the first list of invitees, and acknowledged that her space became available at the last minute.

My mother, herself, had loyal, cherished female friends, yet most of their communication was over the phone. Because she was in her bedroom most days, her bed and telephone became the center of her universe, of my universe, actually, and her 'Mission Control,' where she shared world events and the gossip of others and her own. I often could hear her conversations when her bedroom door was not slammed shut.

With utter shock resulting from her betrayal, I heard her tell 'the aunties' when I had gotten my period for the first time and countless times after. I heard her tell them about

me—my dates, my moods, my need to 'watch it' as pounds
had crept back.

"Yep, it's hard for Barbara. She loves to eat and she knows
she needs to watch it. Now that she has her period regularly, she
has to be even more careful with her weight and the pounds that
creep up."

I couldn't hear the other end of the conversation, but
judging from the amount of time that my mother was listening,
my aunt was giving her some advice. I could only hear mom's
response:

"Yes, she might need to go to a weight doctor. That might
be a good idea. I'll call him."

On so many levels I was appalled by being the center of
her conversation about such personal topics that cut right to my
core, but when I told her how embarrassed I was that she shared
such personal and private information, she laughed and said they
had asked and it was not a big deal. She dismissed me. Barbara's
privacy was not 'a big deal' in my mother's book on boundaries,
but it surely was for me.

While my mother's emotions were sealed off from
me—off limits, to her, my life was a wide-open chapter, which
she quite joyfully revealed to family and friends. She talked more
about me than to me, revealing my joys and my disappointments
with her female friends and family members who would listen.
I so wanted the connection between a mother and daughter
written about in the greeting cards, the ones I gave to her, as
if by signing my name with decorated hearts and X's and O's
would will it so. But, this was not to be. Instead, I, too, learned
to close my bedroom door, filling my hours alone in the room

across the hall from hers. I spent many of my teenage years lying on my bed, listening to the same sad song over and over again, connected and closed off at the same time.

"I am your mother; I am not your friend," she screamed after uncomfortably listening to me lament about my boyfriend frustrations and disappointments. She jumped up from the side of my bed and ran out of my room and into her own room, slamming her door, where she stayed until dinner. There was no apology, ever, not for this frightening outburst or for any other exploding response. When she was calmer, what she uttered instead of regret was, "You shouldn't feel that way," her typical response whenever I shared my sadness. But I did feel that way and many ways—all emotions I learned to squelch deep within. I had no idea that not all mothers reacted so angrily to their daughters' sharing of vulnerable feelings when all I had wanted was for her to listen.

My emotions were too much for her, forcing her too close to the precipice of breaking down, of falling apart herself, of remembering her dead toddler and how she shattered with grief and vulnerability. No matter that I, who took over Jeffrey's place, demanded equal emotional treatment; it was not to be. The way in which she detached from me, the only way she knew, was to cut me off sharply, severely, all at once, which was easier and safer for her yet disastrous for me. The feeling of utter forlornness, complete isolation from so many closed doors stayed with me for decades, molding a self-esteem that became contingent on my mother's moods and the angle of her bedroom door.

Although my mother didn't usually listen to me, she

certainly followed through with my aunt's suggestion to contact a weight specialist. Before I knew it, my mother was driving me to the appointment.

"He's just going to check you out, make sure you don't have any hormonal problems or gland issues. He's supposed to be a really good doctor who knows his stuff. Always good to make sure that you're OK. The aunties know him and he has had a lot of success with his patients."

I didn't quite understand irony as I do today, yet even at 12, I realized something was a little 'off' when I met Dr. Marcus. He was at least 100 pounds overweight. In some recesses of my young mind, the fact that I was going for a weight consultation by a specialist in the field who himself had tremendous issues in this area, literally and figuratively, made me want to shut down even more.

After talking to me, weighing me, which I hadn't emotionally planned for, and taking some blood, Dr. Marcus talked above my head to my mother.

"Have her keep accurate records of her food intake every day. Everything she puts into her mouth, make sure she writes it all down and then come back in three weeks with the log."

I was quite mortified, but on some level, I think that my mother must have agreed that this doctor wasn't the best fit for me. We kept the next appointment, but after it was determined that I ate too much for my size and level of activity, visits to Dr. Marcus stopped.

"Now that we know there is nothing really wrong with you other than the weight, you don't need a doctor to tell you what to eat and what not to eat. You know what to do. Just watch it."

Mother was correct. I didn't need the doctor to tell me what not to put into my mouth. By this time, I had learned to appreciate the hunger pains; the deprivation; the attention from both of my parents when I refused to eat much at meals. No, I didn't need the doctor or my mother to remind me about food. What began as a way to lose pounds based on my mother's assessment became my own secret pleasure—secret starvation.

When my emotions and deemed defiance continued to be too much for my mother, she employed yet another slogan to remind me of her role as life's victim. Actually there were three phrases for one concept: *I must have done something pretty bad to deserve this; I don't know what I did to deserve this; someone must have put an evil eye on me.* While all three phrases were variations on the same theme, the first two were practically the same. Their slight nuances were quite effective and helped nurture my increased sense of remorse when complaining about pretty much anything. After uttering this phrase in response, she would retreat to her bedroom if she weren't there already. She stood at her dresser, looked into the mirror and repeated the mantra, "I must have done something pretty bad to deserve this." Truthfully, we both knew it wasn't what she did, but what I did to her, and what others did to her that provided the foundation for this expression. What I did for her to deserve whatever ranged from not wanting to clean my room; not wanting to wear the dress she chose for me; not wanting to eat her meatloaf to talking back to her about anything; and applying to far away universities in order to live my own life.

What precipitated her utterance of the slogans was never

as severe as her response to me. The bottom line was that I displeased her; I let her down. Basically, her message was that while she had done everything right as a mother, I had failed her as a daughter. Underlying all of this banter and all of these guilt-provoking phrases was what was never articulated, but what I always sensed was lurking not-so-deep-within my mother's mind, *I chose to have you after all I went through, so don't upset me.* These never-uttered words hung heavily within my mind and I became quite adept at plucking them out of my imagination and swallowing them all, one by one, until I earned the guilt that my mother felt I deserved.

And when she decided that life was too much for her, that perhaps I was too much for her, she uttered the phrase that troubled me the most: *Not everyone is cut out to be a parent.*

I really believed my mother wanted to be the best parent she could be. She gave me what she could, but she was depleted, getting through so many days as if she were trudging through quicksand. On mornings when she could barely get out of bed, perhaps a result of a fitful night or fitful thoughts, her body's energy and force had seemingly melted into her mattress. She would get out of bed to see me, walk down the hall, make sure I was ready to go off to school, and then let me know that she wasn't going to leave the house.

"I'm going to spend the day in bed. I'm just so tired," she uttered, as if this phrase, itself, required too much energy to articulate. I found odd comfort in knowing that while I went about my day at school, learning, thinking, playing, eating, talking, she would be in the same place as where I left her eight hours earlier.

During these times when she could barely move under the

dark cloud she denied existed, she would state, "Not everyone is cut out to be a parent." Sometimes, there were no loud voices or hysterics, just a calm utterance, which in many ways was more frightening because it meant that she was thinking, creating an entire monologue of conversation within. So much time to think while she lay in bed provided fuel for her anger and depression. Her slogan didn't always follow a previously held conversation, but I grew to understand it was part of her internal dialogue that somehow found its journey outside of her mouth, often in front of her daughter. I would like to believe that she didn't mean to repeat it aloud nor did she intend the audience to be one of the children who actually helped to create her role in this mantra.

And where was Stephen in all of this? Surely, he was her child, too, so wasn't her slogan about not wanting kids referring to both of us? Stephen knew the afternoons, especially, were my mother's 'off times,' spending hours in her "safe room" with the door closed; he also knew not to enter, not to set her off. But I only lasted so long without opening her door, trying to enter, once again, her world and her heart, so detached from my own.

Stephen saw our mother's 'loose cannon' status as the impetus for his after school get-togethers with friends, always at their houses, creating his vast social life far from our home. Stephen remembers Mother's biting words, often spoken right after his misbehavior, yet her cruel motto held little power over him while I was crushed by such words. By the time I became a teenager, he was drafted into the Navy and soon after married at 21. I became the only child in the house and the repository of more variations of her hurtful phrase.

When she was very angry, her saying became

highlighted, underscored with additional cruelty. Looking straight at me, she commented, "Not everyone is cut out to be a parent. Lots of people shouldn't have children." There was no doubt that I was her intended audience at these times—times when her frustration and anger were boiling over and she had to strike. She sliced my heart in two with just a few strategically placed words.

My vulnerable, young self was devastated by the underlying meaning of her comment. If I were the perfect child, the one she had hoped for, then she would have wanted to have children; she would have wanted me.

What could I really do with the information that not everyone was meant to have children? As a child myself, it meant nothing except for me to wonder, of course, why my mother chose to be a parent.

As I grew, I would occasionally ask her. "Didn't you want children?"

Her response, like my question, was always the same.

"I was expected to be a parent. In my day, there was no question. It was what was done." "And after Jeffrey," she added, "I really didn't want Stephen to be an only child."

I said nothing. There was nothing to say.

My mother's book also included gender expectations—rather, limited female gender expectations. There was complete division of the sexes within our house, right down to bathroom usage. Males, even family members, had their bathroom and we, females, had the blue-tiled bathroom that lay between my parents' room and my own. Of our two bathrooms, my mother mandated the procedures.

"Your father and brother use their own bathroom and we

use ours." While we had our designated lavatories, I loved their large pink-tiled bathroom that, despite the color, was ironically assigned as 'male.' It possessed our only bathtub, so there was dispensation for such use, but if I chose to use the toilet, I had to explain. It just wasn't done.

Gender roles extended way beyond bathrooms and into my academic life. When I struggled in math, Mother reminded me that girls didn't do well in math, so it was okay—normal even—that I had problems in this subject. Even if I didn't believe her adage, I swallowed it, as I did so many other self-foreseeing prophecies. Actually, the only time my sweet father lost patience with me was when he was trying to explain math word problems—trains and planes passing each other at a designated time with my assignment to figure out when they would intersect or which would arrive first. I would have nightmares over these mathematical scenarios.

Witnessing my angst, my nervous mom hired a math tutor. The young math-whiz-college student helped me understand what never came naturally to me, but it was too late to gain back my confidence for numbers and word problems. Between several uncaring, cold math teachers in my earlier years and my freak-out sessions with my father, my inner-script of not being good in math like many girls was written, endorsed and validated by Mom in her Book.

While math unnerved me and reinforced my numeric academic mediocrity, I adored science; biology and physiology became my favorite subjects, in which I excelled. Anything to do with animals and the human anatomy enthralled me, and I enjoyed memorizing every bone and muscle. Sitting atop my mother's bed as she lay under the sheets, my mother tested me on my self-made index cards. I loved these times with her full attention doing what I did best—school work. We were together and she was helping me, yet it was also during these times when Mother reinforced the limitations of my future.

Craving my own mother's compassion and attention in most areas of my own life, it was not surprising, then, that from the time I was a little girl, empathy and kindness were two of my most special character traits. I especially felt for other kids who were excluded on the schoolyard, watching from the sidelines. Like a bird with a broken wing, myself, my limitless empathic nature influenced my desire to help others. In high school, I realized that in terms of a career, my passion for science, coupled with my caring ways, were a great foundation in becoming a doctor. I loved the inside workings of the human body as well as hospitals, and even volunteered for several years as a 'Candy Striper,' wearing the pink and white candy-like-color pinafore that even made my chunky body appear acceptable. I would be a great doctor and get through math some way.

But, my mother shared with me her perspective on female careers; medicine was just not acceptable for a future wife and mother. She insisted that a profession as a doctor would just not work for me.

"You'll want a job where you can still have kids. It wouldn't be fair to them for their mother to be doctor. Plus, you're not good in math. If you want to do something, be a teacher. You can have summers off with your kids and your hours will be the same as theirs. You'll be home with your kids and before your husband so you can get dinner ready."

But, I didn't want to be an elementary classroom teacher;

I didn't want to teach young children; I wanted to help them in a different way. When I asked her about nursing, from my mother's perspective, even being a nurse, while a very acceptable career for women in the 70s, wasn't appropriate for me.

"You would only be cleaning bed pans and doing the doctors' work."

Why, then, did I listen to her? Simply because the volume of my own self-assured voice was muted; I lacked the inner fortitude and confidence to shout back, even internally. I wanted to scream: *I can be whatever I want. I can do anything.* Yet I said nothing. While at that moment I pretended to ignore her comments as I did with many of her one-liners, sadly, I stored them deep within my soul. All of these zingers were irrevocably connected by an invisible emotional thread to my self-esteem and my insecurity, feeding into my limiting beliefs of what I could say and do and be. I allowed her words to define me—to become my own truth, actually believing her frequent mantra to me, *I know you better than you know yourself.* There were only specific jobs that a married woman and a mother could have and medicine was not one of them; I reluctantly, then, by the ripe old age of 15, accepted the fact that I would never be a physician.

I swallowed my own dreams for my future, justifying my new path, veering away from the medical field. By then, when my mother's voice stopped, my own took over, reminding me and reinforcing the perceived truth that I was a poor math student; I just didn't 'get' the concepts of algebraic problems, especially when letters morphed into numbers. Yes, it was a ridiculous, unrealistic dream to become a doctor, especially if I couldn't get past geometry without long crying fests. Most of all, I was happy to please her, to make my life's mission blend into hers.

In those days, I spent no time wondering why I was so adept in my chameleon-like behavior, not just with Mom, but with anyone. I became a Gumby, twisting myself into any shape needed, first, to please my mother, but then, anyone and everyone. My own wants, needs, desires were so far buried within that I ceased to exist. My shadow self, then, took over, casting brightness onto the requests of everyone else, reminding me that I had no needs, only the need to please.

My first 18 years, then, before I left home for college, which unbeknown to me would be a permanent move, were punctuated by our dance—my mother always led and I followed. I longed for her complete attention without caring in what form. I learned to starve and eat again, both emotionally and physically, to study more than I needed to and to earn all A's in the hope that I would be the best in everything, working beyond my potential. I listened to my mother tell me the do's and don'ts from her Book. I displayed perfection on the outside while hiding torment within. No longer could I amuse my mother with song and dance. I replaced my nightly entertainment with foot massages and back rubs, talking to her about my friends, my classes and my day, anything to keep her focused on me. Again, her silent internal alarm would go off. As she lay in bed, she ever-so-slightly lifted her novel in front of her face, signaling my dismissal from her bedroom.

Yet as isolating and detached as my mother could be, there was another side to her—the softer something that enabled me to hold on to the hope that such periods would last beyond hours of such days. One of my fondest memories of these times was upon my return from high school. An over-filled brown

lunch bag lay on my twin bed, the place where Mother left
any purchases designated for me, whether school supplies or
clothing. Perplexed because I hadn't requested anything, I asked:

"What's in there, Mom?"

"Open it up," she grinned.

There, within, were at least 50 gumballs. Referencing her
favorite market, I screamed,

"Oh my God, Mom! You got them from the gum
machine up at the Village?"

"Yep. I took all my dimes and kept turning the knob.
People probably thought I was nuts, but I wanted my baby to
have her favorite gum!"

Mother knew that I craved the sugary chewing gum and
lived for the times when I could go to the machine for one of
the giant treats. Just the act of her driving to the corner where
the machine was located and spending her time cranking that
nob 50 times filled me with utter delight. At times like this, and
there were many, she was contagiously joyful, high-spirited and
just plain fun to be around. It was absolute attention I craved
and while short-lived, it existed enough to know that in spite
of her moods and darkness, she loved me—her only daughter.
These events held the promise of her attentiveness over criticism.

Yet, I needed and desired such attention more regularly,
so I began to search elsewhere, somewhere in a world where only
I belonged, not my father, not my brother, and especially not
my mother. It was a reality they had never known—the world of
college. I, myself, was unclear as to the implications of this life,
but I was beginning to decipher a small voice deep within, one
that screamed "Save yourself!"

I only knew I had to escape in order to protect my soul from completely disappearing.

Chapter Three
Slow Growth

There is no support so strong as the strength that enables one to stand alone. —Ellen Glasgow

Despite my tentativeness in leaving my family (as one of the few members in my extended family who has actually left San Francisco since the 1906 Earthquake and Fire), my inherent desire to grow and experience another life—one that did not possess a predetermined manual—created an unarticulated force within, propelling me to step outside my comfort zone and complete college applications.

I applied to some of the California universities, with my heart set on UC Davis, 200 miles northeast of San Francisco. It was close enough for a family visit, yet it offered me the promise of independence. Quite frankly, while excited to be on my own, I was frightened to such a depth that I couldn't articulate my trepidation. However, I never once changed my mind about leaving home for college. UC Davis was impacted in the early 70s due to its popularity and a growing student population. Therefore, even if applicants were competitive, their names were put into a lottery with every third student admitted. With grave disappointment, I was 'redirected' to the next college on the list, a university in Los Angeles, UCLA, which I had never seen, and had only heard about, with the major attraction for me being its locale of 400 miles from San Francisco.

I had only been to Los Angeles proper when my parents and I would drive down Highway 5 over spring break to visit one of my father's business associates. My reference point for Southern California became the countless tacos I joyfully and guiltily inhaled at the Farmer's Market. I had gone to Disneyland, twice, as a young girl, but that was the extent of my knowledge of Los Angeles—tacos and Mickey Mouse. When I complained about my rejection to Davis, the university officials suggested that I also consider my third choice—UC Berkeley. A small but strong voice within cried: *That's too close to home. It's only across the Bay and in 30 minutes you could be home or they could visit you on the weekends.* I had to consider the amount of miles between my mother and me in my decision in order to have my own life, my own existence. For once, I listened to my own voice. I left both my city and my mother in search of myself.

Going off to college required my mother to amp up her rules and regulations for my life.

"If you have to go to college, make sure you study at the law or medical libraries so you can meet a lawyer or a doctor."

Regrettably, it didn't compute that I could study at these libraries because these were the disciplines I chose for myself, not just to seek a future husband. The degree she had expected for me was my MRS. Degree and told me as much. She was quite emphatic that I needed to meet my future husband at college because, according to her Book, if I graduated without a tangible husband prospect, the odds of my finding anyone after college were very low.

"Barbara, when you really think about it, where will you meet anyone after college? You'll graduate, come home and then you won't be around any eligible men. The time to find one of them is in the next four years. After that, slim pickings, for sure."

I didn't quite know what to say in response to my mother's reminder of the possibility of being an old maid if I graduated without an engagement ring. Yet, I registered her words within the Rolodex of my minimally self-confident 18-year old brain as a reminder that there was yet another hurdle to overcome at the university. I needed both a bachelor's degree and a marriage proposal by the time I graduated. As far as my mother was concerned, only one was required and it wasn't my college degree.

I had no logical understanding that I would be a mere 22 years old upon completion of my four years at the university; I would be just a baby, actually. Yet, the thought of being alone after college, without someone, instilled just enough fear within me to allow her words, once again, to become my truth and my destiny. Initially, her limiting beliefs became my own because I allowed them to be; I wanted so much to live the life she wanted for me. I wanted to please her; that was the bottom line. In the futility of trying to satisfy my mother, I allowed my own being to change direction from its healthy course of expansion.

When I first left for college, my mother's voice boomed loudly within. I accepted my future based on my past. But somehow, I also knew that education was my personal ticket to freedom—not only the freedom in terms of job opportunities and a stable financial future, but education was my way of obtaining autonomy from my mother's limiting belief system. Within a few months of my freshman year, I was slowly, very slowly, able to replace bits and pieces of her mantras, her slogans, with my own. I took baby steps in selecting my classes, my schedule, and my food. I began to carve out a life miles away, where my voice became stronger than my mother's.

Yet, even with my revelations and increasing independence, I was conflicted and homesick. I loved and missed my mother and felt detached from the city of my birth. We talked daily, which helped. When I came home for visits and when my parents came to Los Angeles to see me, I felt my mother's joy in seeing her only daughter. We hugged and kissed and she added,

"I sure missed you, Barbara. It's not easy for me having you away at college."

These words, or similar ones, were repeated with almost every visit, and reflected the complexity of our relationship. Despite my mother's eagle eye of disappointment and her sharp criticism, there was a depth of love for me, layered beneath her hurt over my personal choice of leaving home. I knew, without a doubt, she adored me and I also knew with equal certainty that she was a good person with a kind, empathic heart. It was this mother—the loving and caring woman who recognized her life had to go on after Jeffrey's death—the healthy part of her—that I sought until the day she died.

Such recognition of the best part of her provided me with the motivation to cling to our relationship without ever detaching fully from her. Just as she could be withdrawn and distant, she could be hysterically fun-loving and light-hearted. I clung to the knowledge that both mothers existed and with patience and understanding for her challenges, I loved her with intensity. Perhaps it was the dichotomy of such emotions that enabled me to break away but never completely. I did what I could so that the caring, nurturing mother appeared on the phone and in person while breaking away into my own world of independence. And ... I finally bought my first pair of jeans.

In fact, I bought any garment I could find made out of jeans—besides the pants, I bought a jeans jacket, jeans skirt, jeans hat, and jeans purse. Of course, when I returned home for the summer from my first year at college and my mother viewed my jeans wardrobe, she was appalled.

"Now, you really do look like every other girl," which for me was quite the compliment, yet I paid for my insubordination at our next outing.

"But, Mom, everyone wears jeans. If I don't wear them, I'll look completely out of place at school. No one gets dressed up in nice pants to go to class."

Mom had stopped listening to my plaintive explanation, for in her Book, my new jeans wardrobe symbolized my becoming one of the crowd—my blending in, following every other young girl. Ironically, to me, these pants reflected my breaking away; my determination to own something of which my mother didn't approve; something that was all mine—a way of feeling special. There were so many ways I could have felt special, but I became adept at looking outward for such confirmation—through clothing, through the gifts my mother gave me, through her comments, through the responses of others, and through the secret knowledge of my successful starvation. My mother was a litmus test for my identity and for judging my own place in the world. I gave her that much power because my desire to please her far exceeded my own desire to please myself. The thought that I could possess internal control over my own life was quite ridiculous and frightening; I learned to depend on others' stronger personalities to guide my life and my decisions until I couldn't any longer.

I wore the jeans, but not around her because, as my father would say in keeping with his nautical theme, "You don't want to rock the boat," which was similar to rattling the cage of a sleeping tiger. In our house, we knew that if my mother was not upset, not thrown into a tizzy, then all was well for the moment. My wearing a pair of jeans could set her off if it represented my insubordination. When I visited from college, I learned to acknowledge and balance some of my desires with the ability to keep the peace at home.

Away at school, I could be more of myself—the pieces that I had buried, my unique personality traits came to the surface to observe; I really did have my own likes and dislikes. I was quirky and empathically kind. It was at college, over 400 miles from home, that the realization finally hit me; I had to deal with myself in some way or I, too, would crumble. Even worse, like my mother, I would end up in bed. The jeans, then, became both a physical manifestation and an emotional metaphor in the first steps toward my autonomy, my freedom, and my self-expression.

Despite all of my years of on-and-off starvation, deprivation and fad diets, I was a voluptuous, full-figured, hourglass shaped, junior size 13 by the end of my first year at college. I wore my poundage quite well, secretly convinced my heavy bones added invisible pounds to the scale. Living in the college dormitories, I was gloriously on my own with food. My mother was not there to reinforce my need to cut back and no one, not even I had brought a scale from home, so I felt slightly freer to eat more normally than ever before. Without seeing the numbers, I temporarily tricked my mind into believing that I hadn't gained anything. When my clothing felt tight across my hips and chest, I blamed the dormitory dryers on shrinking my pants and shirts. But, of course I knew the truth. I was gaining weight because I was eating more and as much as I was enjoying every ice cream, donut, and 2:00 a.m. burger and fries that I ingested, I felt a growing sense of remorse.

My slender roommates and new friends appeared to enjoy lots of food—all food. Like a fly on the wall, I watched them eat, not only because they seemingly ate whatever they wanted, but because they apparently weren't really thinking about how many calories were on their forks as they happily placed the lasagna into their mouths. They just ate and laughed and swallowed with pleasure. When my new friends were hungry, they devoured and enjoyed whatever they wanted. I had long since disassociated myself from this natural, satisfying human process in which food was equated with pleasure.

No longer could I open my mouth for just anything and enjoy the flavor, for my mind went immediately to the rising numbers on the scale that I had recently purchased and to my increased pants size, stretching over my chunky thighs. I soon paid the price for my indulgence. If I ate ice cream after dinner, which was easy to do with a 24/7 soft-serve ice cream machine in the dormitory cafeteria, I internally negotiated a plan to skip breakfast and starve until at least lunch the next day. I was always bargaining with myself, before, during, and after meals; it was an exhausting process. I negotiated with pounds I hadn't yet gained or lost and food I hadn't yet eaten.

Then, one day, magic happened without even planning for it, the magic of enjoyment and justification. I learned that if I desired a gooey chocolate peanut butter donut or an 8-inch oatmeal raisin cookie, I could guiltlessly eat with gratification as long as I skipped a real meal to balance out the calories. A 500-calorie cookie was a 'go' if that was all I ingested until dinner. I had almost found a diet Utopia; I continued, then, to make unhealthy choices that would limit or even remove pounds while still guiltlessly enjoying my junk food, never worrying about the harm of such alternatives on a young body. In terms of eating, I almost blended in with my skinny friends who indulged; provided I didn't join them for breakfast, lunch, or dinner. Since I was so good at follow-through, there was no doubt that my determination and my familiarity with starvation played a huge role in my success. I enjoyed excellent internal reviews in knowing how little food I needed in order to still maintain my academic lifestyle of studying hard while utilizing my personal standard of eating.

My boney college girlfriends continued to eat what they wanted without gaining weight. They too ingested the cookies I ate, the ice cream I craved, yet along with the sweets, they still downed extra-cheese pizza, hamburgers accompanied with double fries, and glistening fried chicken with golden crunchy skin. I never understood how they ate all of this whenever they wanted while still maintaining their skinniness, but when they ate, they expected me to eat, too, so at times, despite my plan of intermittent starvation and my internal bargaining, I joined them. They never felt the need to apologize to anyone for indulging in the delicious foods they craved; even more, they never had the need to forgive themselves, a thought that seemingly only entered my mind just then.

No one knew my secret apologies— the torment within my own head, the negotiations, and the deals made between over-eating and denial. Yet, I could manage all of my private debates with a smile on my face and a double chocolate chip ice cream cone in my hand, all the while not just compromising my physiology but my psychology—my loss of a sense of self, all based completely on the rotating numbers on my newly purchased scale.

When I returned home for visits from college, I entered on high alert, as my mother quickly scanned my body so as not to be too obvious in her visual inventory of my bust line, my paunching stomach, my hips, and my thighs. Some time within the early part of my visit, she quietly and gently suggested that perhaps we should take a little shopping trip to get some new pants or a shirt, adding, "Something that doesn't pull." I knew what 'pull' meant, as my extra thickness had apparently stretched the material into bumpy forms for which it was not sewn.

I became ultra-sensitive, adept—at interpreting my mother's sentences with huge chunks of her words missing—her not-so-secret code of telling me I had added some pounds along with my new knowledge. So, it wasn't surprising that when I came home for visits from college, I did some of my best starving. This sequence of events all fit together. I ate more when my mother wasn't around and when we came together, I threw myself into my food-isolation mode, controlling the one area of my life that I could while welcoming her attention, defined by worry and concern.

My time at college helped me in beginning to express my free-spirit nature despite my earlier years filled with my mother reminding me that I was strange. But she continued to repeat what was to become her slogan related to what she deemed 'my weirdness'—*I don't know where you came from.* What she really meant was that I wasn't like her—I was different than she. She had expected us to be the same person, so, my innate personality, which was slowly creeping to the surface, disappointed her. My essence had always been a combination of my father and maternal grandmother's love of people and life, highlighted by an easy-going nature. And just to pour salt on the wound of my developing, distinctive personality, Mom threw a zinger my way,

"And, just to be sure you know, you're nothing like your Nana Bea. I know you think you are, but she never acted this way as a young woman. No way!"

Of course, that comment was a low blow, for I revered my grandmother and often calmed myself with an internal monologue reminding me that while my mother and I were so different, I took after my beloved Nana Bea. My mother did her best to limit such thoughts.

Left to myself at an early age, I probably would have been a hippie. However, the other part of me was the straighter arrow, the one conditioned to want to please adults around me, to conform to the directives of authority figures of all types—my elders, parents, teachers, doctors, and even strangers—pretty much anyone. I was a good little girl never experimenting like some of my friends with anything that could be experimented with. I instinctively knew it would have been quite improbable for me to run wild when I wasn't even permitted to own a pair of

Levi jeans until I left home for college.

Even in this arena, in learning to own my rightful place in my own education, I faced the indecisiveness that plagued me throughout my years; such hesitancy was especially present in selecting a college major. At the university, I wanted someone to tell me what classes to take and what to study, but of course no one would. The counselors could guide and my friends could suggest, but no one knew what interested me but me. At one point, I toyed with dropping out, feeling guilty that my parents were paying tuition for a daughter who lacked direction. My mother would have welcomed my return home, as a higher education, specifically, my own college attendance, was not a necessity or a priority for her. She saw no real need for me to educate myself except to find an educated man. Yet, my father viewed my future differently. Despite the world of higher education being extremely foreign to him, with no understanding of majors, requirements, or general education courses, or any courses, really, my father's advice has always stayed with me:

"Education trains your mind. Just keep on going."

And so I did.

I continued my college education because my own voice within, faint at first, was begging to be set free, to explore, to learn, and to discover. My father gave me the green light and my guilt at spending my parents' money on my lack of direction quickly melted away. I chose, instead, to view my classes as interesting experiences, ways to view myself differently within the intellectual world. My brief conversation with my father became the turning point in seeing myself as worthy of an education. I felt grateful to have such an opportunity and stopped worrying about the outcome.

Yet, my unreasonable vacillation regarding my defined field of study continued, resulting in changing my major six times from English to Communications, to Sociology, to Psychology, to Political Science, until I finally chose the ultimate discipline about which I knew little yet stayed with through graduation and into graduate school—the study of languages, Linguistics. I found one of my passions, which fortunately required no math, on the sixth try and my wavering in my education and career paths suddenly stopped, just like that.

Along with my fascination for languages, actually, my math phobia was a contributing factor in my ultimate decision to study Linguistics. My fear of numbers continued to plague me at the university, by then, an almost visceral terror, but what I lacked in understanding numbers, I made up for in understanding words, syntax, phonology, and so I flourished. Yet, I did not really give myself the credit due regarding the hours entailed in memorizing and becoming proficient in so many different languages—Spanish, French, Italian, Indonesian and Hebrew. Yet deep within, without realizing my growth, I was creating a foundation of academic confidence. I was finally content in my field of study, yet when I felt insecure, lacking self-assurance, not feeling smart enough, I learned to pretend. I appeared to look like the recipient of the grades for which I had worked so hard and ultimately received. I imagined that I was as bright as others in my class, who most likely were imagining the same. I never believed in the other students' unease, just my own. But, actually, pretending eventually worked.

Pretending helped me to *act as if* until I, too, believed in my intellectual abilities. I ultimately recognized that my grades reflected my learning and my learning became a large part of my identity; I was good at it, and completely on my own, I created this world—my academic world. I also tried to ignore questions about what I was going to do after graduation with such an impractical major—languages—and just enjoy the two years of in depth coursework in the various related linguistic fields: socio-linguistics, psycho-linguistics, and anthropological-linguistics. I thoroughly enjoyed most every class I took. I also appreciated having a major that none of my close friends chose to study, nor did they really know what the field entailed; actually being a part of this discipline made me feel special, unique, different. I read about subjects few of my friends enjoyed and in pushing myself so hard, little by little, I began to trust my accomplishments, to believe I could be enough and could be successful.

To generalize, the other students in my classes were a rebellious sort, hippies of the time, and past Peace Corps volunteers, those free thinkers I would have loved to have been if I hadn't been so fearful of myself, so limited in my choices, so afraid to be myself through my own non-existent, healthy and normal teenage rebellion. I somehow understood that my Linguistics classroom peers were free to wear jeans when they were growing up, and to choose not to blend in and to accept what was.

Some of my fellow students were world travelers, lived in Asia, Africa, sheltered in tents instead of trepidation and limitations. I envied them, but just sitting in classes with them made me feel more of myself, more of my own person, and accept my capabilities and my quirks. In college, I slowly transformed into the person I wanted to see in the mirror, not the little girl who was second best at home, but one who could be first in her own academic life.

I found successes in my coursework. I learned the language of academics, and within this world, I built a humble foundation of self-confidence, for it was a world only I controlled, one in which my mother and my past could not enter. While I was tentative in owning my intelligence, never quite forgetting my exclusion from the gifted classes so long ago, I had the opportunity to enter all of my courses on a new footing. None of my professors and fellow students really knew of my insecure academic past and the self-inflicted limitations resulting from being told I was average and believing it all.

I met with my professors, learned how to frame scholarly essay responses and asked for guidance to make my B papers into A's. My professors acknowledged my diligence and rewarded me with their time and attention. I flourished in an environment that belonged just to me, one in which none of my family members understood. In my academic world, I was number one. It was not a surprise, then, that I decided to continue in this self-accepting atmosphere when many students were happy to just finish their four years of college.

While at the university, I also learned about therapy, encounter groups, ESP, past lives, reincarnation, near death experiences, psychics, and astral travel; whatever out-of-the-ordinary idea there was to learn, I read about and talked about. My mother thought I was crazy when she heard me talking about such topics and responded:

"You really believe in that stuff, Barbara?" As she shook her head and rolled her eyes, she added, "Who put those ridiculous ideas in your head?"

My mother then tried to silence me with her frequent mantra, *I don't know where you came from*, reminding me that, despite my excitement, it wasn't safe to share such revelations with her.

But, my father was deeply interested in all of this, asking me questions and wanting to know more. He was so enthralled by my recent session with a psychic that he asked her to fly up to San Francisco to meet with him and some of his buddies. While my mother rolled her eyes at both of us, my father gave my own encounter with the spirit world a level of validity that I just couldn't produce by myself.

My mother would frequently ask, "Why do you want to know about these things?"

'These things' stimulated me … the unknown, the realization I had much to learn in all areas of life, finding my purpose for being. I felt as if my leg braces had been removed and I was running in all directions—so desperately wanting to experience what I had only read about. I came to realize that I wasn't weird at all. I wasn't a kook, but someone who was passionate about life and wanted to fill all of my days in meaningful ways, learning about what I hadn't known before— learning about myself. Once I tested the waters of my own interests, there was no going back.

My time at college, 400 miles away from home, provided me with exciting revelations to pursue, not only in my linguistics major, but also in sociology, psychology, and anthropology.

When I spoke to my mother on the phone, she would ask how school was and I learned to say it was fine. That was the response she wanted to hear. My mother inquired about my boyfriends, what I wore to parties and to whom I spoke. These topics were safe and ones in which she wouldn't remind me how weird I was. My father was interested in the details of my psycholinguistics classes, of the African click languages I studied, and my professors. I learned to adjust and share the details with others, and only told my mother what she wanted to hear. My college education gave me so much more than a degree; I reclaimed the inquisitive child that I had been so long ago and became comfortable in asking my questions, knowing who to ask and what answers I could share with my family to avoid my mother's perennial question as to where I came from.

After college, I never returned home again to live permanently. Ironically, in leaving for my own survival, I destroyed any possibility of true closeness I could have had with Mother, for she never forgave me for leaving—for leaving her.

"Daughters aren't supposed to leave their mothers; sons maybe, but not daughters. No family member has ever left the Bay Area except you. And certainly no daughter has left her mother."

I broke my mother's cardinal rule—perhaps the main one in Her Book—of a mother-daughter relationship. In referring to her own mother, my grandmother, she asked me, "Where would Nana be if I had moved away?" My mother was quite proficient at rhetorical questions that were all variations on the same guilt-ridden theme, repeated to me throughout the years. They ate away at me while reinforcing the fundamental fallacy that I wasn't a good-enough daughter.

It wasn't in my mother's life plan for her only daughter, the child she was forced to exchange for little Jeffrey, to live her own life and to live it far from her own. My life, actually, was supposed to be hers, an intangibly sealed contract she must have internally negotiated with herself when she reluctantly agreed to give Stephen a live sibling, especially a sister. I envisioned her secret monologue: *If I have another child, especially a daughter, she will do what I say and when I say it and live where I want her to live.* While she never uttered these exact words, throughout our lives together, the implication for me was so very clear.

From an early age, I felt my job was to make her life easier, to complete an unattainable task of healing the broken parts of her soul shattered by the loss of her baby boy. In not living in the same city as my mother, I broke her heart and she truly never forgave me. Unbeknownst to me, and despite the miles and her failure in keeping me in close proximity to her life, she did her best to orchestrate my life to be near hers.

On one of my visits home during my last year in college, I found a letter from my past love-at-first-sight boyfriend Jack. We had met at a friend's wedding and we instantly came together while he was in San Francisco. We were in love. When Jack flew back to Chicago that summer, we continued to talk and write, sharing our thoughts and love, making plans to visit each other. I began my first year of college and he began medical school, but after a year, the letters stopped, as did the phone calls and his plan to visit me at UCLA. Jack's mistake was that he sent the letters to my home address, not to my college address. He gave up on our relationship when he believed I had stopped responding to his letters. My mother never told me that the letters had arrived nor did she share that she had intercepted them, forgetting to throw one away—the one that I had found.

I incredulously asked her why she had kept the letters from me, allowing me to believe that Jack had just stopped caring.

"I didn't want you to end up in Chicago," was her simple answer that justified her behind-the-scenes work against my possible future and, most important, a life far from her own.

In time, Jack faded into the background of past loves. I fell in love again, several times, while at college, but I fell in love for good when I met Paul, who just happened to be in medical school. Paul always put me first, which meant everything to me. He was also everything I was not—self-assured, independent from his family, and positively opinionated. His admirable self-confidence helped mine to grow over time. He knew what he wanted and what he needed: family, a career with upward mobility, a home, and travel. These were the very elements I wanted so badly, so the healthy part of me, the young woman screaming for independence and growth, fell in love with Paul, the man holding such promise for a complete life. My soul sensed what I could not accurately articulate. Paul made me feel whole even when I knew so many of my pieces had crumbled. Throughout our very long marriage, just as I had hoped, these fragments have come together, strengthened by Paul's constant devotion and his unwavering support.

When I walked off the plane three months before my college graduation for a visit home, before my mother acknowledged my physical presence, before she embraced me, she immediately grabbed my left hand to see the diamond engagement ring that Paul and I had chosen. She was beaming, and as a diligent student in all areas of my life, I followed her directions; I got married exactly one week after graduation. If I couldn't become a doctor, at least I married one. She did not attend my graduation because she was too busy planning our wedding.

"The aunties found your wedding dress at the Emporium."

Not once did I find anything strange in my mother's emphatically declarative statement. I was living in Los Angeles and my wedding was in San Francisco, so I had not even considered shopping for my own wedding dress nor did I plan one element of the wedding except to make sure my friends were on the guest list. Joyfully, and with great relief, I allowed my mother to do everything without even thinking I could and should contribute my thoughts to the wedding process. My frame of reference was always to defer to my mother and I never questioned whether it was normal for the bride to be so disengaged in the process. The bottom line was that I truly didn't know what I wanted and what I liked; it was enough for me that I knew whom I wanted to marry. I left everything else up to my mother, thinking that was what good daughters were supposed to do. I had no involvement in my wedding nor did I think it was strange that I was yet again a bystander in one of the most pivotal days of my life. My future husband felt otherwise.

When I flew back up to the Bay Area a month before the wedding, I tried on my aunties' discovery—the $99.00 off-the-rack stark white dress, which I deemed 'just fine' even if it was the only dress I tried on. Once again, I wanted to please my aunties, my grandmother, but most of all, my mother. How could it be that I, the bride, had no real opinions about my wedding dress let alone the entire wedding? I entered my marriage in this same way. I thought having no definite opinions was normal, that I was normal. Paul did not understand my undying devotion to a woman who could be loving and jovial yet at the same time cruel and detached to his soon-to-be-wife. He quickly figured out that as the new kid on the block in our family, he was well advised to quietly defer to Mother and let me deal with her. He was lovingly protective over me while I clearly chose my mother over him in most interactions.

In my Mother's Book, men were supposed to be disengaged in the wedding process as well as all matters on the home front. However, Paul had opinions, as most healthy people do, but because he was a man, my mother made it clear to me that he shouldn't care about planning weddings and household-related business. He certainly should have no voice in choosing dishes or decorating. While Paul was far more artistic and interested in planning than I, he learned quickly not to share his opinions regarding the wedding details.

Sadly, I provided no go-between, no support for my fiancé. He realized he was on his own in engaging with my mother. He let many wedding-related issues go, but he put his foot down with the selection of our dishes. When Paul accompanied me to see my choice of a white porcelain background filled with flowers, he was appalled.

He stated in no uncertain terms, "I can't eat off these for the rest of my life. There are bugs all over them."

In my non-observant way, I had overlooked the creepy crawlers—the ants, ladybugs, and caterpillars. My mother was immediately upset that Paul cared about the plate selection and I was upset because she was upset, the usual chain of reaction in our relationship dance. My mother took me aside in the store and whispered:

"What's the matter with him? Why does he care about which dishes he eats off of? Men don't usually care. You pick what you want. That's the way you do it."

But, as was my usual response, I just shrugged and felt sick inside, for I really didn't know what I wanted. Maybe I didn't like the insect dishes after all. What did it really matter? I deferred to Paul and we chose another pattern.

While I changed the dishes, I also acquired another notch on the buckle of my low self-esteem. I was not even capable enough to select the appropriate plates for our new life together, and from my mother's point of view, I was not competent and strong enough to stand my ground with my soon-to-be husband and keep my original selection.

Her only comment was, "I didn't raise you this way."

Her disappointment lay in my deference to my husband, as she raised me to defer to her, not him.

And so as a 22-year old, I began my married life. I went straight from living with my parents, to four years of living with my college roommates, to my new home with my new husband. I had never lived alone. Even more, I found myself married to two people—my new husband and my forever mother. As a new couple, I barely made room for Paul between my multiple daily phone calls and constant emotional connection to her. From my mother, I sought a blueprint, how-to directions, for my role as wife. Despite the hundreds of miles separating us, I was as connected to Mother as if I lived down the street.

As a newlywed, my mother offered me one piece of advice, "Make sure to clean the bathroom every day."

This was her sage support for my Los Angeles wedded life. My keen ability to read between the lines of her seemingly benign bathroom guidance restored my guilt and inadequacies in not having played a bigger role in wanting to permanently return to Northern California. Thus, I literally spent the first three years of our married life crying every night. I would kiss Paul goodnight and go into our den to shed my tears, for I wanted to live in San Francisco, close to my mother and the rest of my family who had never left The City. I wanted to be with her, to show her I could be the daughter she needed and wanted—the daughter she was to her own mother; most of all, I believed I needed her guidance in more areas of my life than just sparkling bathrooms.

My sister-in-law Marilyn shared with me that when she married my brother, on her wedding day, her own mother reminded her that from that day forward, her priority would be her new husband and their one-day family. Right before I walked down the aisle, my mother reminded me not to forget where I came from. She wasn't referring to the city of my birth, but rather the essential reverence to her—that she should always be the most important person in my life, and she said as much. Yes, my mother provided me with a far different message than the advice Marilyn received.

Never forget your mother, who must come first—the

clear mantra of my mother's chapter on a mother/daughter relationship. I sadly listened diligently for so many years.

Looking back, I was lucky Paul stuck around and waited for me to grow up. Of course, it was terribly wrong of me to choose my mother over my husband, but as was the case with many issues in my life, I chose the path of least resistance. It is testimony to our life together that we are still together—he made room for my mother, sometimes reluctantly, but nonetheless, he did so when another son-in-law would have understandably pushed her out of our lives completely or at least issued an ultimatum. Paul loved me unconditionally and was willing to wait for me to change—to grow a backbone. My mother, on the other hand, was more than able to cut me off for hours, days, and weeks. That, I couldn't bear.

Paul loved me so much that he was willing to share me, or just borrow me, a process I negotiated with a big price—my self-worth. Sadly and honestly, it took me many years to realize that my own family came before my mother. It took me even longer to realize that such a choice should never exist. Again, what saved our marriage and my personal development were the 400 miles between my mother and me.

With Paul's help, I slowly learned to view my mother's responses more objectively and I began to grow up within my marriage. Paul and I learned to look to each other and to spend more time together, undiluted by family or other responsibilities. Actually, the truth is, without my mother close, I learned to look to Paul for many of the answers, instead of my mother. Paul even taught me to ask important questions—to question what I had always accepted as 'right'. I also realized that, like my own mother, Paul not only had opinions about our selection of dishes, but on countless other issues—he had a voice and used it. I emulated him and learned to argue without withering away and to state my opinions—never to my mother, but to those who were safe—Paul and other family members and close friends. Living far from home, I slowly carved out my own life. Yet, I regressed almost completely during each of my parents' trips to Southern California, reverting immediately to the mother-dependent little girl who I had worked so hard to extricate between visits.

"You're so different when you're around your parents," Paul reminded me.

This seemingly hurtful statement was completely true once I acknowledged my defensiveness and admitted that his perceptions were, of course, quite accurate. My mother's comment to me during our time together would often reflect her observation of what she believed was my stunted emotional growth, "Where is Barbara in all this?" suggesting, quite ironically, that I had lost my identity to my husband when it should have been to her. When my mother was around, I lost my voice and my internal compass pointed only in her direction; I allowed her that much power over my life.

While I made great strides in my independence, I also defaulted to the comfort of not making decisions. Because of my imprint, because of my limited self-confidence in my own choices, because of my almost pathological need for approval and to please, I often deferred to Paul. It was easier to give in, for his self-assuredness trumped all of my insecurities. Paul knew how to decorate our apartment; he knew how he wanted to spend his free time; and he knew what he didn't want to do; and most of all, he articulated these thoughts and feelings with the certainty that I lacked.

When we rented our first apartment two months before our wedding, Paul moved in right away and set up our new home. During this time when he lived there without me, he organized the furniture and meticulously placed our paintings on the walls. He knew where everything should go better than I did. While I was deeply disappointed in not having more of a say in how our first shared apartment looked, in retrospect, I lacked confidence in my own opinions, resulting in my vacillating over the most mundane issues and decisions. I did not have the strength back then to speak up or make any decision—even a poor one, but at least it would have been a decision. And, I then got angry with Paul for not anticipating or knowing what I was thinking. Sadly, I had learned indecisiveness, so making no decision became my strategy.

As a young girl, I deferred to my mother, allowing her to make decisions for me as I grew, which created an unhealthy selflessness. This process of deferring to Paul and my holding resentments began unknowingly, yet it often defined many years of our relationship. I was lost in the equation of indecisions, by my own making, and it took decades to reclaim my voice and my rightful place in my own life. I allowed this emotional takeover to happen.

As my mother's daughter, I permitted myself to disappear and reclaiming my individuality has been a painstaking journey. At this late stage, I am finally coming into my own, learning to accept and even more, honor, my own wants and needs at a time in life when many have no problem saying and doing what they want. For me, every day presents a new challenge in decisions. Do I do what I am supposed to do as an earnest wife and mother and friend, or do I do what I need for my own life regardless of what they all think? My indecision, vacillation, and hesitancy are the legacies of deferring to others, of sliding into second place, of people pleasing, of looking for validation from those who cannot give, of not ever feeling that I am doing enough or being enough.

I dutifully memorized my mother's chapter on what type of wife she wanted me to be—an outspoken woman who was in charge of everything, even her husband—but not, of course to her own mother. But, that was her role as wife; I was the opposite and it bothered her terribly. At the same time, she reminded me yet again of my chosen role as daughter —one who left her own mother to go to college, never to return home—one who just didn't care enough to sacrifice absolutely everything in her own life for her mother. I was like a yo-yo, being pulled up and then thrown back down. I felt loyal to my mother and wanted so to please her, yet I was married with an obligation to another relationship. I was tormented in this wishbone-like existence, with both entities pulling at me as a reminder of where I truly belonged. I ignored and buried my own needs and desires with remorse and guilt steadily surfacing.

No matter how good a little girl I was growing up; how successful I was at school; how I managed to find the requisite husband before college graduation; and how content I was in my life, I chose to make my married, adult life in Los Angeles, so I had failed her. In her Book, the chapter about mothers and daughters reinforced the belief that I was not supposed to have my own life; I was supposed to have her life. Shaking her head, she added:

"I should have never let you go to UCLA," she would often say. "I paid a heavy price in your going away to college."

I didn't have to ask her what price this was, for I knew it wasn't the college tuition. As my mother saw it, I permanently left her. And just as a reminder of my mother's grand disappointment in how her life had turned out as a result of losing her only daughter to a new husband and a far-off city, she would end many of our phone conversations with, "I'm here and you're there." While I had no response, such a comment reinforced my emotional IV-drip filled with guilt.

Chapter Four
Motherhood: the Voice Strengthens

Truth cannot only comfort you. At times, it has to cut through to the bone, to the very marrow even, if this is what it takes to set you free. —Mooji

Becoming a mother was my great equalizer, the literal moment of reckoning, when my wavering had to stop, at least for decisions affecting my children's lives. There was another life depending on me, so I had to choose, I had to decide, and I had to judge—and most of all, I had to have an opinion. I had to respond for the good of my children. My initial wake-up call was in the hospital right after giving birth to my first son Michael. I attempted to breastfeed, but I was very awkward and nervous, worrying whether my constantly crying baby was getting enough milk, assuming I was doing something wrong, for the process did not come naturally to me despite the pre-natal classes I took and the books I read. I attended these classes diligently, but when the baby came, I apparently flunked. Within hours, I asked the nurse for a bottle of formula, but then, riddled with guilt, I tried breastfeeding again, to no avail. My internal conflict grew.

During the week I was in the hospital, recovering from surgery, the card on Michael's bassinette under 'Choice of Feeding' had a list, appearing like a scorecard, with 'breast' and 'bottle' listed and crossed out countless times. Finally, the pediatrician paid me a visit, instructing, almost demanding, that I make a decision, as I was making the nurses crazy, not to mention, confusing my baby.

Clearly, my indecision reflected the torment of my feelings of inadequacy. I didn't want to make a mistake, hurt my baby, so instead I continually changed my mind, waiting for someone to tell me what to do, yet as the mother, I was supposed to already know or at least have an innate sense. I possessed neither. A young, militant La Leche League female came into my hospital room to tell me I was poisoning my baby through the formula I was giving him. I cried, feeling like a failure three days into motherhood. I looked to my own mother for support in this instance, but she only stared back at me, incredulously, with her response, "How should I know?" I assume if my own blueprint for parenthood was faded, she found hers even harder to read.

My first labor culminated in a C-section, but not before 40 hours of labor, trying to avert the surgery. Apparently, I had flunked my Lamaze classes, too. We agreed with our doctor who suggested that we not tell our families, who were waiting hours in the waiting room, about the decision to have surgery until it was finalized. However, my mother couldn't wait anymore and stormed into the labor room, yelling, "I can't take this anymore! What's going on?" Granted, she was extremely upset that I was having problems in the delivery, but the focus, as usual, was on what the situation was doing to her. She waited for me to come out of surgery and then left. I never saw her the next day, for she was too distraught to come to the hospital to see her new grandson or her daughter.

She was 'stretched out' (a term she used throughout her life, reflecting her supine position in bed combined with her intense mental anguish) in her hotel bed, recovering from my surgery. She said I had made the wrong decision... that I should have told her right away what was going on. What should I have decided? What should I have told her? No matter what I did, it wasn't up to me to make her feel better during my own labor and delivery, yet the remorse I felt was enormous. On what should have been one of the happiest days of my life, I felt isolated and inadequate yet again. I apologized to my mother for her experiencing my extended labor and tortuous delivery. I didn't make the right decision and she frequently reminded me.

When my mother visited me after I came home from the hospital with Michael, I greeted her at the door of our apartment with him in my arms. I wanted her to take him, to relieve me of this incessantly crying baby, whose immature digestive system caused him pain and colic. I did not know how to comfort him which further fueled my maternal inadequacy, evidenced by my panicked expression and honest comment, "I feel like throwing him over the balcony." I was at wits end with a baby who wouldn't sleep and after what seemed like hours in his taking the bottle (despite my guilt, I gave up on breastfeeding before leaving the hospital), he would burp and spit it all up, only to start the entire feeding process all over again. I was on edge with a lack of sleep and a lack of my own maternal instincts.

My mother's sobering response was direct: "There's something terribly wrong with you."

She was right; my mother's invalidating reply to my exasperated, desperate comment left me feeling even more inadequate, for she already knew what I accepted—I was an incompetent mother. Why I continued to confide in my mother or sought empathy from her became my life's rhetorical question, yet I already knew the answer. If I continued to show that I needed her for every part of my life then she would want me to be in hers—our dance. I was the ridiculous, inept young mother still wanting the support of a disapproving mother.

One of my first realizations of my motherhood came to me soon after I took Michael home from the hospital. For the most part, I was mothering based on the mother I knew—my own. I truly had no imprint as to what to do with a crying baby who never stopped, but I was willing to learn—to learn anything to make my baby love me, to stop his crying, to be at peace. Do I hold him? Dr. Spock's book on babyhood and parenthood said to take care of his physical needs and then let him cry. Do I go against Dr. Spock? My own mother, when I asked her again for her help, told me she had no idea what to do with such an unsettled newborn. She truly meant what she said when she could give me no words of wisdom in calming Michael.

Yet, my mother's compassion for our crying baby was infinitely supportive and endless; while she did not attempt to ease my frantic, new motherhood apprehension, she did whatever she could to help Michael feel better and stop crying. She ran to the market, to the pharmacy, getting any suggested remedy—a special pacifier, chamomile tea, special formula. She diligently sought out whatever was needed with the joy of being on a mission. We gratefully appreciated such a reaction, for what she could not give in my emotional support she helped us logistically, cooking meals and helping me in my physical recovery from surgery.

She lovingly added: "I am taking care of my baby so you can take care of yours."

I responded with gratitude and concern for her own exhaustion, "But you must be so tired. You haven't even rested today. Do you want to go back to the hotel?"

"Don't worry about me. I'm going home soon. I'm here to take care of you and help you out." And, she meant it.

Interactions like these reinforced my mother's inner strength and loving heart. Such caring words reflected the other side of my mother that came out more and more with Michael's arrival and with his subsequent brothers. Some of the awkwardness reflected in our own interactions was never present when she was with her grandchildren. She was warm and loving, deeply interested in all areas of their lives and generously patient with them. While she wasn't the type of grandmother to get on the floor and play with the kids or even take them to the park and throw a ball, she was an incredible grandmother in what she could give emotionally. I was overjoyed in her consistent love for them, showing me yet another side of a very complex woman who I both loved and feared.

When my mother left to return home, Michael's suffering continued and I tried everything to relieve him of his discomfort. At the same time, I made his tortured days about me—I wasn't the right mother for him; I shouldn't have had a baby; I must have done something wrong because he wouldn't sleep. I saw other babies peacefully sleeping in their cribs, in their strollers, and in their mothers' arms, concluding that all of these other mothers were better at motherhood than I.

Days of his fantastic alertness, sleeplessness, and projectile vomiting wore me down until I was sure that I was being punished for some karma the universe was righting in this lifetime—again, it was about me. Early motherhood, punctuated by my emotionally unsupportive mother and an incessantly wailing baby, reinforced my belief that I would never be a good enough mother. I noticed other mothers' relaxed smiles as they walked around the outside world. I, on the other hand, once again felt as if I were carrying a huge secret. I loved my baby, but I was a deficient mother. My phone conversations to my mother were always plaintive and filled with a complete loss of what to do to calm my new baby.

"He wasn't that bad when I was there. Eventually he calmed down. I really can't help you, Barbara. You and your brother were never really like that. I never had a baby cry so much. Maybe it's something you're doing wrong. Do you think?"

Of course, this was exactly what I thought and my mother's question hung over my days reinforcing my own new parental inadequacies. Even Paul seemed calmer with our screaming baby and certainly more empathic over Michael's digestive pain. I wanted to be a mother so much, yet I never expected I would not be able to soothe my wailing newborn. So, besides my mother's question pounding within my own mind, I created my own: *What kind of my mother was I?*

But, within weeks, in spite of what I did or did not do for him, Michael grew out of his immature digestive system into a smiling, laughing, giggling, contented baby. And just like that, I became a better mother, but the legacy of memory I carried throughout my entire child-rearing days reinforced the notion that I just wasn't good enough. Way beyond the early weeks of his incessant crying, Michael's actions—how he behaved or didn't—became a direct reflection on me, as if we were one in the same people. I did not contemplate, early on, that he was completely his own little person, coming into the world with his own DNA and personality. My continued internal punishment was a lose-lose formula:

What he didn't do well was because of me and what he did well was in spite of me.

As he grew into a precocious, joyful toddler, it was evident that he was exceedingly intelligent, quick, bright, witty.

"That one is a handful, Barbara. You'll be busy with him. He's smarter than you are," added Mother.

I only smiled, appreciating the fact that he would never have to endure an inner, nagging voice reminding him of a limited potential. I also knew he would never have to experience the overused, limiting set of words that defined his mother's view of herself; he would never hear the slogan uttered to me by his grandmother: *Middle of the road is good enough.*

Less than two years later, I was pregnant again. When son number two, Adam, arrived, he slept and ate, cooed and slept again. I was sure that something was terribly wrong due to his continuous peacefulness. I looked up his 'condition' in Dr. Spock's book on childrearing and was just as sure that Adam's quietness was unhealthy until my best friend and sister-in-law Marilyn tried to comfort me:

"No, Barbara, that's what babies do. They sleep and eat."

Marilyn, who was only four years older than I, was ahead of me in the parenting journey and light years ahead of me in her comfort regarding motherhood. This young and very giving woman, a brunette with a peaches and cream complexion and hourglass figure, was confident in a multitude of ways that I wasn't. She entered my life when I was 14 and quickly became my genuine older sister, my guru, listening to my every problem and issue when my own mother decided she had heard enough. Whatever Marilyn told me about motherhood, I knew was the right information.

Having no internal understanding that my new baby's tranquil personality was obviously a gift and quite normal showed me that I lacked an inner motherhood compass that Marilyn so naturally possessed. So, I tried to strengthen my maternal weaknesses and skills by reading whatever book I could find on parenting. But any encouragement I felt about myself and my mothering skills was diminished instantly by a negative comment from either my mother or my mother-in-law, sending me back to the beginning of my new, inadequate parenthood days that had been punctuated by a colicky, fretful baby. I took their words as gospel, as truth, for I had a limited internal mechanism that registered that I was okay; the negative voices from the outside always provided overpowering voice-overs for my own.

By the announcement of baby number three, my mother just came right out and said what was on her mind,

"I can't take this anymore. Haven't you heard of those surgeries they do now a days?"

Incredulously, she was referring to a tubal ligation so that I would not have any more children. So that I wouldn't have been able to have this new life within me!

I responded: "Where would I be if you had had that surgery?"

"That's different," she replied. "That's not nice, Barbara," referring to my inference of her lost son. "I only wanted two children."

My replacement child legacy was again defined by my mother's perception of her own daughter's motherhood, another role in which I could not quite get right. But, as usual, I was a brilliant decipherer of reading between the lines and what she communicated non-verbally as a response to my question was quite simple:

You wouldn't have been born.

In my own quest to be a loving mother and in the search for my self-esteem, my own motherhood helped me to understand that there were actually two versions of love. I acknowledged that just because I was angry at my little boys, I still loved them, regardless of what they did. Through my own emotional hard work and the support of my husband, I learned that the adoration between parents and children can be pure—a love that is created unconditionally in wanting the best for that little life, now in the charge of adults. What I didn't quite understand for decades was that the love my mother had for me, while intense, was conditional and her rules kept changing as I changed, as I grew into my own person. Despite feeling that I wasn't a good enough mother, I gratefully had the one qualification that any suitable parent needs—the ability to give and to feel unconditional love.

This quality should have provided me with the confidence knowing that as long as I was emotionally present for my boys and did my best in taking care of their needs, that everything else would fall into place. However, I continued to torture myself on a daily basis, always searching for the answers in a non-existent mothering manual, questioning whether I was doing it right—defining 'it' as everything. I lifted my maternal bar so high that I could have never attained the degree of success that I believed other moms innately possessed. Of course, I was wrong. I was just fine, but it took me years to realize my maternal strengths.

I constantly sought support from the outside, for I couldn't judge myself as to whether I was doing enough as a mother. I needed validation from someone, but little children don't acknowledge that their parents are doing a good job, so I had no one in my life to reinforce what I so desperately needed to hear. I kept searching for the answers and for someone to confirm, yet no matter what I did, I never measured up to my internal gage of maternal precision.

Of course, like my eating disorder that entered my life full force at countless times throughout my life, my perceptions of my deficient mothering skills were constantly on my mind, tormenting my days with my own questions that I could not answer: *What are you doing to make your boys act the way they do? Why aren't you relaxed with your kids? Why don't you know what to do? Why can't you just 'be' and enjoy?* I was frozen by my own continuous questions.

Something within sought further torture, for despite my mother's inability to support me in my own motherhood anxiety, I kept asking her for advice. My mother had infinite patience for her three grandsons, yet, for me, she was quite limited in the tolerance she doled out. Her comments and judgments only reinforced what I already knew.

"Snap out of it, Barbara. Figure it out. You know what to do. Those kids are fine. It's you who needs help."

Even my mother-in-law added her own unsolicited advice when she visited:

"Take Brian's blanket away. He shouldn't have it at seven years old. Adam needs to go on a diet. What are you feeding him? Michael acts fine with me. He only acts up around you."

I felt bombarded from both ends, with no backbone to stand up to both of my mothers and tell them I was doing the best I could. Again, I said nothing aloud, but asked myself the same question that rose to the surface whenever my maternal deficiencies were highlighted: *What kind of mother was I?*

I played with dolls until the age of 14, so when it was time for me to be a real mother, I felt that my long-ago joy in my baby dolls provided the foundation for my strong, innate parental instincts. However, my insecurities as a mom of a real child prevented me from just being and enjoying my sons and trusting these instincts. I loved them fiercely, but my fears of making mistakes, of doing something to permanently mar their psyches, prevented me from relaxing, from truly enjoying so many moments with them.

I was so concerned with being the best mother and wife, making sure the house was together, the meals cooked, and my children socialized, that while I tried to emotionally feed everyone else, I left a mere internal shell of myself. I perceived myself as insufficient in countless ways. Whatever anxieties I possessed as a single female and then as a young wife were nothing compared to those I felt as a young mother. With no foundation for an internal recognition of what to do,

I was drifting in unchartered waters, navigating with only the unwavering love of my little boys to keep me afloat.

When my three little boys were very young, my mother reminded me of yet another one of her mantras that she must have been saving for just the right time: *Mothers of sons are selfish.* Since my mother had a son, I wondered why her slogan, didn't refer to her, too, but she clarified her definition, "No, Barbara, only sons—Mothers who only have sons." I questioned her so-called statement of fact and she responded:

"Oh, they think only of themselves before their kids, maybe because they don't have another female in the house to focus on. They think about themselves first."

Then, my young-mother mind ran down the list of women we knew who only had sons. I repeated each of their names and asked Mother whether they were selfish. Then, I realized that this definition included, the mother of my father and my uncle.

"Even Nana Rose?" My beloved paternal grandmother, who always brought me See's suckers when I was ill, who was eternally loving and sweet to me.

"Especially, Nana Rose," my mother emphasized. "She thinks of herself before any of us."

Perhaps my mother created this adage specifically for her kind and caring mother-in-law. "Well, I'm not selfish," I stated, as if to remind my mother, but she only responded, "We'll see."

Instead of dismissing this ridiculous saying, I considered my narcissistic fate. In my mother's pearls of wisdom, she was, in fact, telling me that I was self-centered, self-absorbed, and selfish, three traits that no one has ever used to define me, except my mother, who again stated that she knew me better than I knew myself. Her ridiculous comments about my selfishness became a turning point for me, fueled by my anger and disgust at anyone thinking I was self-centered, especially my mother.

Thus, in my early 30s, I finally changed the equation of my marriage, something, of course, I should have done from the very beginning—from our wedding day. I finally put my husband before my mother. The shift happened subtly, at first, almost imperceptibly. It began when I asked Paul what he thought about countless things, what he wanted to do, and then I asked my mother. Our shared parenthood was the reason why I deferred to Paul over my mother. We were on this challenging journey together and only he knew my darkest thoughts and did not criticize me for any of them, for he, too, had his own. We grew up together in our marriage and in our parenthood. Our three children were our family, not my mother's, and while it took me far too long to recognize this, it wasn't too late. Paul's loving patience was the reason why I could safely separate from my mother's reach that had even extended through the phone and across the miles between us.

Yet, I still refused to become a statistic of my mother's slogan, so I warded off any chance of my own motherly selfishness. I became even more vigilant in attending to everyone's needs. My little boys, of course, came first, followed by my husband and then my mother.

I made sure to take care of everyone else except myself. Once again, I was swimming upstream in a sea of guilt. I did not dare focus on what I wanted. I had no time and little disposable income; plus if I were to do anything for myself, I would be deemed selfish, especially because I had only sons.

Whatever emotional support my boys needed, I made sure they got; I was far down the list of my own priorities.

While I naturally thought of others, my mother's adage reinforced my need to pick up the pace of my nurturing and supportiveness. I was exhausted, fighting against my own needs. I began to neglect myself and my nutrition; my energy suffered. Early motherhood and my fear of becoming one of those mothers of males who thought only of themselves was eating away at me, a perfect breeding ground for my own eating issues to surface yet again. In fact, I defined myself by how much I did for others even when I didn't want to and how little food I ingested as further punishment for my male-based fate of selfishness. How sad that, left alone, I was just fine. I had inherited my father's nurturing disposition, so there was little danger of my becoming one of those self-centered females—ever.

As my motherhood years unfolded, I forced myself to ignore the slogan when it popped into my mind because, quite frankly, I was at the other extreme of selfish—I was selfless, bringing with it its own neurotic actions and repercussions. A decade after I finally put my husband before my mother, another piece of my life's puzzle came together. I realized that Mother's motherhood male mantra was really about her—about what type of mother she was to my brother and I. And, her indelible phrase had nothing to do with the gender of her offspring. It had everything to do with who came first and it wasn't her son or her daughter.

As a result of my newfound inner strength and my determination to see myself as a good enough mother, I also gratefully acknowledged how differently I reacted to my own children than my mother did to me. In fact, during an earthquake in Los Angeles, I responded in a very different way than my mother did when I was three. When a Los Angeles trembler struck, I immediately collected my toddler in my arms, where he stayed for what seemed like the rest of the day. My maternal instinct, actually, focused on protecting my child, not running from him. To my mother's ironic defense, I was actually talking to her on the phone when this Southern California earthquake hit.

After the phone service restarted, she called back to see if everything was okay, and her first words were, "Get the baby. Do you have the baby?"

Perhaps she had reflected on her own choices 30 years previously when she left me on the living room floor and ran for cover.

It was a fascinating dynamic that took place while raising my boys, for she loved them unconditionally and provided them with limitless smiles and hugs and kisses. In fact, for each of them, she created her own special connection.

She could get Michael out of his moodiness by simply reminding him that she hadn't gotten one of his "emergency hugs." Within seconds, his sullen face turned into smiles as he ran to her for just that. She never disengaged from him with the slight push I remember her giving me when she deemed to have had enough of such an embrace. Instead, she clung to him until he was ready to let go.

Adam loved to create elaborate productions with characters and show bills. Mom sat through all of these impromptu performances never once looking at her watch or uttering what I had grown accustomed to hearing, "That's enough." She clapped the loudest and always ended with the same remark:

"He's definitely going places. You'll see."

Brian, the youngest, became her last-born grandchild. As a little boy, he loved books and the two of them would sit for what seemed like hours reading and rereading some of the same passages. Again, Mom never once ended their special time together herself; instead she waited for Brian to complete the last page of his book.

For her grandsons, she had infinite time and patience for which I was so grateful. I was happy that they received the type of love from her that I would have wanted but that she could not so easily give me. If I ever complained to her about what they did or didn't do, she was the first to remind me that they were normal.

"They are typical boys, Barbara. Leave them alone; they are fine."

She especially liked to reiterate this last piece of advice, for she saw them as separate little people from me, their mother, and in this healthy view of her grandsons, she wanted me to understand that they had their own thoughts, feelings, likes, and dislikes. The irony was not lost in her desire to have me separate from my own sons yet not from her.

Her tolerance and understanding were quite frankly awe-inspiring and I am grateful that my boys have so many positive memories of a grandmother who they legitimately recall as loving and giving. This is as it should be.

Today, if you ask my sons about the type of mother I was, their remarks might be generally positive, or so it seems to me when we interact. Of course, they have stories and each their own perspectives of their childhoods, but I assume that my overall grade would be at least passing with the knowledge that despite everything, they have always been deeply loved.

Still, I try not to reflect on what I could have done differently if I had just believed in myself. Instead, I view myself as a good-enough mother who loved empathically and unconditionally. I regret the existence of my self-inflicted daily torment, for my dreadful self-abuse would not have occurred, and this would have made all the difference in my own life. I can say that I did the best I could under the circumstances, but perhaps I could have survived unscathed had I learned to trust myself, to see myself as enough.

There was a seemingly 'forever-space' between giving birth and watching my three sons choose the most important women in their own lives. Through huge pockets of this vastness, I experienced motherhood with extreme limitations; so many times I just didn't know what to do or say. Yet, mothering never stops even when actual child rearing does, and no one really knows the anguish I feel, even now, in my interactions with my boys. Today, my boys are men and are completely on their own. They have women in their lives and each looks to his partner as the most important female in his life, as he should. I am careful not to invoke in them any degree of guilt, the kind that was infused by my own mother, guilt that began long before my wedding day and continued throughout our mother-daughter relationship.

I would never place such a heavy burden on my sons, yet, deep within, I have a pain that I try to eradicate, try to release.

I did not realize that in giving them all I had, I would also have to give them up. I raised three little boys, giving them everything I emotionally possessed, and the end result is that they appear to be content, empathic men who are able to show healthy love and devotion for another person while making their own way in the world.

My lesson is to learn to love lightly, to let them go ... to be satisfied with the connection we did have and do have. Yet, I cannot deny that I feel as if I have become a second-class citizen in their lives; I say this with nothing more than pangs of longing, and with no invocation of remorse or infliction of guilt. It is the realistic realization that they have new lives, chartered in a different course than where they began, without their mother directly accompanying them.

I am the one who must accept their healthy growth, the growth I dreamed for them, yet there is an old tape playing within, reminding me that I am not good enough to be in their lives any more, validating my perception, yet again, of a not-good-enough mother. I understand the irrationality and dysfunction of my words, not mirrored in reality. So, even with adult children, I am constantly playing an internal game of not measuring up, when the only person whose validation and acceptance I still truly need continues to be my own.

I had always wanted children, I knew this for sure; I had also, quite frankly, wanted a daughter, someone to acknowledge all things feminine, including me. Ironically, this was one desire that my mother reinforced quite often, and couched her comments in phrases that reminded me that even in this arena I still didn't quite measure up. While I wouldn't trade my boys for anything in the world, with every male to whom I gave birth, my mother commented, "I knew you'd have another boy" as if she believed I had lost the gender lottery. When we were together, she would comment on a 'beautiful family' she had recently seen—one that included a girl and a boy.

"Look at that little girl," she would point out, continually reinforcing my almost instinctive desire to feel complete by having a daughter, of which I yet again fell short.

Of course, having a healthy baby was all that mattered, but when the dust settled and I had my complete family of three little boys, all under 5½, I knew that there would never be a daughter in my life without the words 'in-law' attached.

Other women have daughters, but you just can't seem to have one, once again, coming in second, was my mother's repetitively implied message. Sadly, I accepted this perception as a fact, knowing I hadn't quite measured up even in the gender category of my children.

Having daughters-in-law, despite how wonderful these young women are, intensifies my replacement child syndrome, for while I know I have an important place in their lives, it is a place that I need to stay as second best—a second class mother. I will never be as cherished as their own mothers, and, intellectually, I completely understand this, for I felt the same way. To be a mother of sons is to lay all of the groundwork—the foundation and the architecture—and not live in the ultimate magnificent creation, to be the visitor and the outsider on an inside project.

Despite my role as an under-the-radar-mother-in-law, and having been acknowledged as a wonderful one, perhaps due to my low-maintenance requirements, I will always be the replacement mother; the stand-in; the second in command; the second babysitter after the official maternal grandmother has bowed out. This self-inflicted torment, although lessened at times, continues.

To add to my maternal feelings of inadequacy, I made the mistake early in my motherhood passage to not share my own emotions and moods with my sons, primarily because, as a child, I had had enough of my own mother's volatile nature, enough of her sharing. She imparted her thoughts and feelings readily while raising me and they were mostly not pretty. While her laments were too much for me to handle, at some point early on, I unintentionally agreed to manage and protect her feelings while disregarding my own.

Thus, I decided early on that I would never burden my boys with any of my disappointments and my struggles. They would see a finished product, the impossibly perfect mother, someone who was almost always happy and at peace, someone who was always there to help them, and someone who never needed their help. In orchestrating my role as a low-maintenance mother, I deprived them of not seeing me the way in which they should have seen me—as a three dimensional human being with foibles and desires and needs. I did this to them, but mostly, I did this to myself. I felt worthy only when attending to their requests, and discounting my own less important needs. Even as a mother, this became my replacement child legacy… to stay under the radar of my own existence, so that I wouldn't, metaphorically, be returned.

Consequently, I have three grown sons who really don't know their mother, an inheritance, of sorts, that I sadly offer them, by my own doing. In wanting to please them, in hyper-focusing on their needs, I robbed myself of my own, which so long ago didn't seem important or relevant. To no culpability of their own, today, my sons aren't used to having a mother with her own wishes and desires or life.

In not wanting them to agonize over supporting me emotionally, as I did with my own mother, I denied them the experience of really knowing who I am, and most of all, I have sadly denied myself of this relationship. This is my motherhood legacy as a young mother who began parenthood feeling not good enough and as a seasoned mother who still struggles with feeling less than.

While one, of course, is always a mother, my 'active' parenthood journey is now on the waning side of life, and my years as a daughter to my parents, sadly, are officially over. I am a wife who has lived more than twice as long with my husband as without him, defining this relationship as a toasty, worn, comfortable, old robe. We know each other so well that at times we find our safe corners and agree to disagree, but always with an undercurrent of love and respect. We have been very lucky in our lives together, but we have worked at this good fortune. We have weathered countless storms, many surrounding our children, and while we have emerged scathed, we have emerged together.

Despite my self-inflicted motherhood torment, the end results are, quite frankly surprisingly positive, for my little boys grew into lovely young men, but how would I have known of such a favorable outcome decades before? The consistent torment I put myself through resulted in severe harm to my spirit, a legacy of not viewing myself as a good-enough mother, when, in fact, I always was.

Chapter Five
Learning

*The beauty of empowering others is that
your own power is not diminished in the process.*
—Barbara Coloroso

Immediately after my wedding, then, I jumped into a two-year master's program. I did more than enough in every class to earn my A's, studying overtime, probably unnecessarily. As soon as I graduated, I began my career teaching English to adult second language learners. Perhaps my inspiration to teach English in a non-traditional classroom, to non-traditional students, related to my joyful memories of the multi-national seamstresses of my father's shirt factory so long ago. Like these dedicated women who loyally sewed shirts and ties for our family custom shirt business, my motivated students came from almost every part of the world; I lived vicariously through their sharing, for I had never really traveled. They taught me about multi-culturalism; gave me an understanding of their experiences of culture shock; and showed me how to connect beyond languages and differences, through kind, passionate, and joyfully patient teaching.

Throughout my years in the classroom, I was enough and not an insecure daughter, wife, or mother. There was only one teacher in the class and in this setting, I was clearly number one. The act and art of teaching came quite naturally to me and it was my true calling—my passion. My mother did not understand my need to work, but when it came to my teaching, I actually didn't care what she thought. I was my students' respected professor through the sharing of my knowledge, which they were actually interested in obtaining. I began to take their lead and listen to my own voice, too, truly believing that, at least in this one area of my life, I had the confidence in knowing that I was a very effective instructor. I knew I could help them improve their lives through their mastery of English. What I was doing mattered and made a significant difference to my students while strengthening my self-worth in ways that no other area of my life could.

I prided myself in creating this new world completely as a result of my own education. My people-pleasing personality provided the foundation for me to give 100% in the classroom, so this quality, born out of the internal need to prove my significance (and existence) in the world, actually worked to the benefit of my students. My desire to be the greatest instructor, better than anyone else, propelled me into the arena of 'favorite teacher' semester after semester. For me, it was a win-win situation and I actually received Distinguished Faculty of the Year for my tireless and boundless pedagogical energy. I loved my students and wanted to make them happy; my students adored me and appeared to learn the information I gave them while enjoying the classroom environment I had created. With grateful humility, I was in my element.

Of course, I recognized that my students provided me with the positive, almost constant feedback that I was missing in other areas of my life. My students showered me with small gifts from their homelands—statues, scarves, coin purses, foods of all types, but their appreciative words, often written in cards, were the most meaningful. They told me I was their favorite teacher; that I was the best teacher they had ever had; and that their writing skills were greatly improved because of my instruction. I needed these words of appreciation, which became my encouragement for working even that much harder. I made myself available to them on nights and weekends and I made sure that whatever they requested, I did my best to give them. For them, it was a win-win situation to have a teacher so interested in them and so willing to go the extra mile. For me, it became an exhausting fete, always feeling I could do more and be more. Basically, I needed their approval and feedback; the more I obtained it, the harder I worked for it.

So it wasn't really surprising that in addition to my teaching, I worked as tirelessly for the college's campus as I did for my students. I participated in every faculty committee available. If I gave 100% of myself inside the classroom, if possible, I gave equally outside of the classroom. I became a whirling dervish of energy and non-stop work. Administrators noticed; if they wanted something done, they only had to contact me, for my reputation, of course, was one of never saying 'no.' I worked on weekends and after hours, sitting on hiring committees and participating in off-campus events. My elixir, to which I became addicted, was the positive reinforcement of the occasional administrators' comments related to my indispensability. I became both the best teacher in and out of the classroom. Yet, I misconstrued the attention I was getting from administrators as their confidence in my abilities. Yes, there was that, but basically I was a warm body who was able, ready, and more willing than any other person to do the job—any job presented to me.

I even wondered why my colleagues were not interested in doing such validating work. I thought there was something amiss with them; it took me over a decade to understand that there was something wrong with me—with my thinking. Yet, the more tirelessly I worked, the more the division dean grew to depend on me, asking me to take on even more responsibilities outside of my teaching, which meant time away from my students but more confirmation of my importance to him and the office. I agreed because I misinterpreted his additional requests as affirmation of my exceptional work, needing to believe that I was the best faculty member ever. I sadly wanted his approval and for him to like me the most; that was the bottom line. And so, slowly at first, I worked more in the college's division office, reducing my teaching hours by half. I saw myself as indispensable in working with the dean, the support staff, and in helping the faculty while still in the classroom. I held the two positions at 50% time each but slavishly did whatever I was asked, giving much more than the equivalent of one full time position.

"What would I do without you, Barbara?" was all I needed to hear from my supervisor in order to keep up this intense pace. I needed the accolades this much; my supervisor quickly learned that such simple, positive remarks, scattered throughout the work week, were the only incentives I required to do my work—his work.

It took me far too many years to realize that my need to please was often not altruistically accepted by others; instead, my constant work, punctuated by my positive nature and good intentions were taken advantage of by my supervisor and other supervisors, by faculty, and even by students. The common denominator was me—I allowed my craving for constant praise to be more important than my self-acceptance and even more important than the realization that I did not actually enjoy office work. But by the time I understood that others held no additional good will toward my tireless endeavors, I had logged countless hours on this people-pleasing treadmill. It took much self-reflective humility and inner courage to leave the job that I allowed to define me, to fall from grace, which is what I eventually did, but not before my final academic climb.

I really can't say when the idea entered my soul, but this lightening bolt awareness within was the determination to return to graduate school in my mid 40s to earn my doctorate. Professionally, I did not need this degree. I was comfortably ensconced in my joint teaching and administrative positions and really had nothing to prove to anyone at my college. Personally, I had more than enough to do, especially while most all of my working friends had their nights free to join book clubs, relax at home, or get together with other friends and family. Along with my full-time job, I still had two of my three boys at home, and a very ill father I frequently visited in San Francisco. At this stage, I could have chosen to take my life easier, but my journey has so often been about proving to myself, testing my self-worth, validating my abilities, working overtime within the confines of my own life.

I was my own worse critic, raising my own bar so outlandishly high that I always fell short of my own expectations. I personally sought the accomplishment of a doctoral degree as one final way to prove that, once again, through my learning, I could be enough, see myself as enough. If I couldn't earn my medical degree, I could at least obtain a doctorate in education. And so I did. It was that simple and that complex.

I completed the requisite application to graduate school; I dealt with the graduate entrance exams; the humbling process of obtaining letters of recommendation after decades of absenteeism from academic higher education. I wrote the obligatory personal essays, selling myself and why I should be admitted, never forgetting that I was competing with many applicants half my age. Once again, I was determined in this goal; I needed the acceptance letter for many more reasons than merely to acknowledge my new academic status. Several months passed before I received my letter welcoming me into the UCLA education doctoral program. My three years of graduate work, culminating with the highest academic degree bestowed, provided me with my final frontier of achievement in academia—the equivalent of having been admitted into the Gifted Program so long ago on the first try.

My mother just shook her head and said, "What do you need this for in your life?"

When I explained to her that it was a gift I was giving myself, the final chapter in my educational career after so many years, I could have been speaking Greek. She had no appreciation of my personal need to challenge myself, to push myself, to test myself.

Again, she just rolled her eyes, shook her head, and questioned my sanity, as she added, "What does Paul say about this? Certainly you'll have less time at home. And the boys? It's really not fair to them. Selfish, actually."

I stopped defending my decision and didn't give her the satisfaction that Paul wasn't thrilled with my choice either. In fact, Paul thought I should wait longer, until our three sons were out of college, themselves, until we had paid for their education. Of course, logically, he was correct. I already had my time—my opportunity decades ago when I could have made the choice, before children, before so many responsibilities to others, to continue beyond my Master's Degree. I wasn't able to make such a commitment then because I was in a hurry to teach and at the same time, start a family. I also had such low self-confidence and didn't believe I could have successfully studied for my doctorate. Paul made a good case for waiting; in fact, very few people responded with the remark I was looking for: *That's great, Barbara. Good for you!* Many just didn't quite understand why I would commit myself to projects, papers, exams, and a dissertation at this point in my life. But, I knew that if I didn't at least try, while I was still in my 40s, I would never again have the opportunity and that was what I wanted to do—more than anything.

While my mother deemed my return to graduate school a self-centered decision, it was perhaps one of the first times that I took my own needs into consideration and refused to listen to anyone who tried to deter me from my goal. Mother, especially, never appreciated that despite my two previous graduate degrees, I was still living with the feeling of being 'found out,' of others realizing that I was just 'average.' It wasn't until I was in my doctoral program did I consider that perhaps the IQ test administered decades earlier could have been incorrect or, at the very least, falsely limiting. I had since studied the concept of multiple intelligences and knew that I could be smart under these new categories, perhaps just not only under the traditional one measured by numbers, spatial figures, and outlandish vocabulary pairs.

I was half way through my first year of coursework before I even began to acknowledge the substantial quality of my own writing, again reinforced by outside sources, for I still did not fully recognize my prose potential. When several of the professors requested my permission to use my 20-page leadership essay as a model for other students, I incredulously agreed.

Even after so many years, was my writing that strong that they wanted to have the other students read it?

After this and other similar requests, a seed of confidence began to grow within and when a well-known professor in the field of writing agreed to chair my dissertation committee, again, I felt an inner strength regarding my academic accomplishments. I told myself that he wouldn't have agreed to work with me if I couldn't write. Once I began to trust that my writing was actually something others wanted to read, my excellence became a self-foreseeing prophecy. I wrote more and my colleagues and professors provided very positive feedback; some of my peers actually sought my input for their own papers.

By the end of the first year in the doctoral program, a simple phrase entered my mind: *I can actually do this.*

The momentum of confidence increased until I became

the first in my class of 30 to file my dissertation; in fact, I did so on the actual day of my 50th birthday, the ultimate gift to myself. I felt personally and academically vindicated in countless ways, so much freer from the past negative, limiting voices, which provided a restrictive self-placement to which I know now that I never really belonged. Yet, I was the only one capable of freeing myself from these self-inflicted constraints, and I did so but not without a tremendous amount of physical hardship and substantial academic work.

For three years straight, I spent almost every night and weekend, either at home or at the library, working on my courses and then my dissertation, all the while holding down a full time job and caring for my family in addition to my monthly visits with my parents in San Francisco. My doctoral work was my final frontier, my final academic experience in which I agreed to twirl the dishes in the air in order to prove to myself that I was actually as worthy as others who seemingly never needed such relentless, intellectual proof—or any proof at all.

Although my father died six months before, Mom was quite emphatic when I asked her if she was coming to my graduation:

"Oh, I'll be there, Barbara. I wouldn't miss your graduation for anything. I'm so proud of you!"

I knew she meant it.

And, like my mother often did at times that punctuated essential elements of my life's defining moments, my mother eagerly attended my doctoral hooding ceremony despite the logistical challenge of getting there from San Francisco. While she could still walk, she accepted a wheelchair due to the uneven grassy terrain of UCLA's grounds. Mom was front and center along with Paul, my sons, other family and friends—all cheering me on.

Mom was clearly perplexing, as she was never a champion of so many of my out-on-the-limb choices, often made to improve the quality of my life. Yet once she saw my commitment—when I wanted something for myself without a doubt—she supported me all the way. Sometimes complaining and questioning, she nevertheless became one of my main cheerleaders. Nothing about my mother was predictable or even shades of gray—they were black and white, which I grew to understand and accept as I, myself, aged.

Upon completion of my doctorate, I was jubilantly determined to become a leader on my college campus, a full time administrator, who would work tirelessly as a champion for other faculty as I supported the campus initiatives, always with the focus on the students and their needs. However, after leaving teaching and obtaining the position, I found myself a committee of one, for many of my fellow administrators, unbeknownst to me, purposely kept a low-profile, not wanting to do any additional work or actually anything innovative. For them, the status quo was acceptable within the four walls of their offices. They looked at me as if I had come from another planet. I had no idea I was fighting an uphill battle, which I would ultimately lose. Many of my administrative colleagues did not want to represent the faculty, nor did they really want to represent anyone at all. When the vice-president asked me why I wanted to be a dean, I told him I saw my role as one who supported faculty.

His simple, shocking response has always stayed with me, "What do they need support for?"

Even with his diabolically opposed values, I chose to work for this man for two years, for I sadly needed even his acceptance that much.

My fall from grace at the college, then, was in slow motion, but a fall nevertheless, seen by other administrators as a huge black mark on an otherwise unblemished career. For me, though, it was my eventual ticket to inner freedom, the final time when I removed my work-related people-pleasing shackles. While I went into administration for all the right moral and ethical reasons, my naiveté and my selflessness could not prepare me for the power of negative, mean-spirited people and their abilities to derail my dreams of making a difference in the institution.

At first, I assumed my new position with many surrounding smiles, as most of the college community—faculty and other administrators—wanted me to get the job. I was to be the conduit between the dean and the faculty; I was to field student problems and report to the dean. I continued to chair countless committees and meetings. I became so good at what I did that the Vice-President, the same small-minded man who asked me why I wanted to be a dean, took notice and called me into his office, asking me to work for him. Of course I said yes, for yet another person needed me and wanted me—the elixir that kept me going. It took me two years in this position to finally understand why I was selected.

At first, I had really believed that, like the dean, the vice-president admired my expertise, but I had the one major qualification that enticed them both—I was a workhorse and could do my job and theirs. But, eventually I admitted to myself that to continue working for this man would be untenable, for I could not sublimate my own values and principles just to keep another person appeased, especially someone who did not deserve my goodness.

When I studied leadership styles in graduate school, I identified with the type of leader who helped others realize their own, full potential; I was committed to doing the same and champion them along the way. How ridiculously innocent of me to believe that other administrative educators felt the same. Certainly there are many who believe in helping others, for that is the major reason to become an educator, yet there were only a few at the institution in which I was working.

Other faculty who knew me well were thrilled I was in this position and I mistook their excitement for a personal connection. While they questioned why I would want such a position, they were glad, at least, that I did. They knew they couldn't communicate with the dean whose door and mind were often closed to their complaints, their successes, and their daily teaching schedules. I, then, became the person to whom all of these issues could be directed and discussed. I felt so connected, so needed; I mistook compliments of my work for the teachers' friendship, and their daily conversations, for caring. Basically, the teachers needed a job done, and I was the warm body to get it done well and quickly—and always with a smile.

My first realization that I was not viewed as someone very special in the position of Associate Dean was when a well-respected professor, whom I admired, saw me from the other side of campus and came sprinting toward me with a smile on her face. I actually anticipated her thanking me for the amazing job I was doing on behalf of the entire faculty. Instead, she asked me if I could reimburse her for a stapler she had purchased. All my education, all my years of teaching, my hard-fought interview process, my leadership skills and training, all came to this—payment for a stapler. She never even said hello; she only wanted her ten dollars.

My final 'ah-ha' moment, the one that provided clarity for my superfluous role as a dedicated administrator among those who didn't care, came one early morning upon my arrival on campus. As I was on my way to enter the three-story Humanities Building, thousands of gallons of water came pouring out of the doors, literally, a flood. Apparently a hot water pipe had burst on the second floor and flooded all of the first two floors—the teachers' offices and the hallways. Some of the classrooms were affected, but most of the damage was in the teachers' offices and the connecting hallways.

The vice-president, the same man who singled me out as his willing assistant, the same man who couldn't fathom why faculty needed support, was called at home to come onto the scene to assess the damage. Even though I was the appointed disaster captain for the building, my leadership was apparently only needed for the annual earthquake drill. The vice-president made the decision to keep the building open and to hold classes, never considering that the teachers' materials and books were submerged under chemically treated water. Of course, I shared my concerns for the faculty and the students, but he did not listen and no one else in a position of power did either; I was a lone voice. No one considered our disabled faculty and students who could not navigate the building or the air, which had taken on a chemically induced smell, making it hard to breathe as the day progressed.

At this moment, the floodgates opened in my own mind, and I attained such clarity; no one in a position of power concerned themselves with the welfare of the teachers or the students, just that business should continue normally, that the college should continue to generate income from attendance. To make matters worse, after the flood had subsided, the college president came to our office to speak with the dean, bypassing my office for the emotionally detached administrator who had done nothing during this disaster except to arrive three hours after it began and then thanked me for taking care of it all. Upon his leave, the president passed by me and spoke to me with his only reference to the flooded hallways, "I am most worried about the carpets matching." He was referring to the two floors of ruined carpets; his priority was to make sure the carpets could be replaced to match those in the rest of the building. With displaced faculty and students, and potential health concerns, his two articulated priorities were color-coordinated carpets and to rename the flood 'a water leak.'

This flood, then, ironically became my metaphorical and literal watershed moment, showing me a few of the people I was really working with, those who thought so little of not only my tireless, genuine work on their behalf, but of the community of educators and their students—the reasons why the college existed. So, I completed the academic year, and left my administrative position, with the vice-president using the word 'defection' when he announced my departure. My 'defection' became my ultimate release from the people-pleasing chains at work. I welcomed my return to the classroom, to my students, to working for those who appreciated my devotion and my genuine, caring ways.

Upon my joyful return to the classroom from the negativity of administration, I also finally accepted myself as an exceptional instructor; I assumed a new role—a professor who knew her own worth. No longer did my insecurities seep through into my teaching. I diligently knew how to communicate the process of writing. I did not question my interpretation of the literature nor did I believe, as I once did, that others analyzed prose and poetry much better than I. As long as my heart was in the right place, as it was in all of my life's roles, then my students were getting the very best from me. In placing many of my insecurities in their rightful place—deep beneath, I was able to 'act as if' so much more easily. And, in 'acting as if', I learned to believe the validity of my calm demeanor and my excellence at my job.

Then, five years ago, I obtained some proof as to how far I had come in my self-esteem when I came across a comprehensive IQ test sold in a bookstore. While official intelligence tests are administered by professionals, this was my 'everyman's' opportunity to vindicate myself from *middle-of-the-road* status. I was surprised that my hands became clammy when I picked up the box filled with directions and test questions. Clearly, I had been harboring the trauma of the earlier test and results. After all these years, I needed to purchase the kit—I needed to do so for my own piece of mind; I needed to learn the truth that had defined my restricted intellectual abilities so long ago.

Uninterrupted, I took the entire test, following every direction. The results indicated that I could have joined Lori's class in third grade and that I wasn't *middle-of-the-road* anymore. I allowed my mind to wonder, thinking that I wouldn't have had to internalize that slogan during my school years. I could have entered so many classes free of the dread that I wouldn't understand the material. I wouldn't have had to go through school with my shadow self, wondering which professors would find out the truth about their average student and eventually acknowledge poor Barbara, who was working to fulfill her limited potential.

I have many friends and family members who inherently know they are smart with the same assuredness as they acknowledge their eye and hair colors. I have never had this core belief, the default position that reminds me that I could have an off day on a test or paper and still know that I am smart enough to complete the class. For me, I was always waiting for the final shoe to drop, the one that reinforced what the professor had probably surmised after receiving my first essay submission. Yes, she is just *middle-of-the-road*. It has been an uphill climb for me, almost clawing my way into acceptance of my strong intelligence. Even now, when I write this, I hear a voice saying:

Aren't you presumptuous? How do you really know you are so smart? You are so full of yourself.

One might argue that my lack of confidence in this area actually worked to my benefit, for as a student, I never procrastinated; I recognized that I needed every waking moment to complete my homework. I never pulled all-nighters in my studies as some of my friends did, for I felt that I needed time to process the material and then test myself on everything all over again. If I were given five days to write a take-home exam, I used all five days, planning the hours meticulously with plenty of time for writing and rewriting.

For decades, while I worked hard in fighting against this limiting belief, I allowed it to define me—my intelligence, my academic abilities, my overall acquisition of knowledge. The words were always in the back of my mind, surfacing when my confidence waned, when some mean-spirited professor would comment on my work in a less than positive way, as if he, too, knew my mother's slogan and the real truth.

Today, I have worked tirelessly in creating a new slogan to replace such limiting beliefs. As an affirmation and even a mantra, I tell myself I am smart, but more than intelligence, I also remind myself of the qualities I like best about myself. My compassion, empathy, and kindness have guided my encounters, my teaching, my mothering, my life. My abundant common sense and patience have served me well in all life-related situations.

I finally understand that I came into this world with my unique gifts that do not need to be measured through a standardized test. Once again, I have had to nurture the part of me that grew up, in a sense, with metaphorical braces—limiting me from rising to my full potential and abilities. I have tried to make up for lost time. My words to myself are the slogans I needed to hear so long ago, for no one I know—family members, friends, most of my students and even I—have ever been *middle-of-the-road*. And, even if I were average, ordinary, common, I do not have to be defined by such qualities, for I am so much more.

But, I also acknowledge, at times, that I am not able to see myself in the ways that others might view me. While I have a doctorate in education, and my students reverently call me by my professional title, there are times in which I actually forget I have earned this degree. While I can always clearly recall the endless hours of writing and reading, the exams, and presentations, I often forget it was I, alone, who worked diligently for this accomplishment. An experience I had soon after I earned my degree sums up my own lack of awareness in many of my attainments. When the phone rang, the UCLA caller asked to speak to Dr. Jaffe.

"Oh, he's not at home," I responded, not once thinking that they were calling for me … that I, not my husband, was the Dr. Jaffe to which the call was directed.

Quite interestingly, my replacement-child legacy created unanticipated fodder for a successful teaching career. Simply, my need to be liked and appreciated compelled me to give my all to each of my classes with no sign of burnout. I have earned the trust and love of many of my students through mutual respect and my ceaseless work. They notice my abundant patience and my passion for teaching. An old voice tells me that I still could give more and do more; I am always so much harder on myself than on them, or anyone.

As a teacher, myself, I also pay tribute to a few of the horribly negative teachers from my past who reinforced my insecurities through the need to sharpen the knives of their own dull egos. My high school Spanish teacher, when seeing my tentative hand-raised, frequently responded: "Are you going to ask another stupid question?"

His question crushed the remaining slivers of my fragile self-esteem, as I stopped asking questions completely, with my low grade reflecting his beliefs and my own fears. Actually, I learned much from this teacher and several others who used their power in front of their classrooms as weapons to humiliate and tease, to discourage rather than inspire. My high school Honor's English teacher, after reading my first essay, suggested that I wasn't 'Honor's Material,' and sadly, without any internal resilience, I believed her words; I allowed them to define me and I stopped writing for over a decade, just like that, for I was that fragile.

Oh, how I wish that I could have been a different type of student…a young girl who could have used such words to propel rather than to recoil; to prove the teacher wrong; to generate an inner strength. I eventually vindicated myself, but not without enduring far too many years in the shadows of such internalized, destructive comments.

As a result of my own demoralizing earlier classroom incidents, I have chosen the opposite type of teaching— compassionate, empathic, and patient, reminding my students that all of their questions are important. I took my own damaging encounters and created positive lessons to share with my students, ultimately learning, myself, that I did not have to be defined by the cruelty and shame imparted by deceptively refined individuals.

I share my past discouraging stories with my students, using my own spirit crushers as ways to reinforce the idea that no one has the right to define us, to limit us. No one, I remind them, has the right to tell them what they can and cannot accomplish, to take away their dreams, but really, I am reminding myself. Today, I choose not to engage with deceivingly smiling faces, which under the guise of support, subtly offer limiting, belittling, and destructive comments. I have slowly learned to free myself from such negative energy.

My developing writing students often enter my classroom with palpable trepidation. They dislike English and have had negative past experiences in learning the subject, ironically, like my own. I remind them that they can choose not to have these comments define them as well. It is a choice. I also remind them that they can be successful in learning how to write, for writing like any activity is a skill that takes practice to acquire. I tell them that they might not write the great American novel, of which I have not yet either, but they can learn strong writing techniques to be successful in their other classes. For most everyone sitting in my class, this is their goal.

I choose literature that speaks to my students, prose that help them learn about themselves as they write their own stories. At the end of one class, a student posted an evaluation:

"Dr. Jaffe is amazing! She is not just an English professor, but a professor of life... I'm not only better in English but a better person."

I keep this comment on my desk to remind me of my potential impact on others, especially when my insecurities surface. After 16 weeks in my classroom, my goal for my students is for them to have a new way of thinking and feeling about themselves and the world, as this student so beautifully articulated. I see myself in them, some so fearful, so tentative, so detached from their own brilliance and potential, and I hope to be the conduit to their inner strength, that when nurtured, fuels their writing and their personal growth.

As I walk into a classroom, I can easily experience the same joy and the apprehension I once felt as an inexperienced instructor three decades ago. Now, instead of being younger than my students, I am as old as their grandparents. My age does not concern me, however, for my energy has not yet waned. And while my continuous desire to strive for excellence has resulted in my placement at the top of the teaching popularity pole, within the last few years, I acknowledge that I don't have to be the best teacher, that there are others who are equally as strong, many stronger, and I am fine with this. I don't need to be 'the best' any more in teaching, or in anything; actually, I finally understand that good enough is just fine. Most important, though, when my own vision of myself as a professional clouds—the one that considers the job and the title I have earned, I can see myself more clearly in my students' eyes and this sustains me.

I am finally enough.

In leaving my family for the university, an anguished young girl with an eating disorder and a fragile self-image, I ultimately found my self-esteem within my academic and professional careers. Teaching others to find their voices through their writing has ironically given me my own in ways that have often eluded me as a wife, mother, and daughter. It is not surprising, then, that when I applied for my full time position over 25 years ago, my mother asked me with incredulous disdain, "What do you want anyway, *a career*?"

How ironic that I should find myself in just that! As my mother's daughter, I was raised not to desire such an achievement. Yet, my own glorious, decades-long learning has afforded me the immeasurable gift of finally putting the pieces back together, of finally being enough in my own eyes. In this one area, at least, I do not view myself as second best or runner up. I studied hard and the tangible rewards were my strong grades and three academic degrees, yet more than the parchment on which my degrees are written, through my learning, I have accepted myself, a gloriously unexpected and priceless gift. Education gifted me with a complete emotional ticket to my inner freedom; truly, books have set me free.

Chapter Six
Slowly Reappearing

Our deepest wishes are whispers of our authentic selves.
We must learn to respect them. We must learn to listen.
—Sarah Ban Breathnach

It is a gift to view oneself as enough in a world that seeks more from everyone and everything. Like the unacquainted image I have of my reflection, my internal adequacy gage cannot quite regulate; it is always more than slightly off, yet age has given me the ability to accept what I cannot quite repair. While my strengths and challenges are not all a result of my position in our family as the replacement child, the dynamics that catapulted me into existence played a tremendous role in my arduous goal toward self-acceptance.

While Stephen and I came from the same family, his early unequivocal and unencumbered welcome and his first six and a half years of life were quite different from my own, during which time the seeds of my 'not good enough' legacy were planted. My standing in the family provided the perfect storm of my approaching every day with something huge to prove. When I was young, the proof was to my mother, but as I have aged, it is to myself, at times, an equally unforgiving audience. For countless years, my mother's image of me became the one that reflected in my own mirror and colored my days.

While my own arrival was joyous despite the circumstances of timing—one baby dies and another is soon after born, I have remained skeptical of such pure recounted elation. My perceptions, either based on reality or interpretation, have presented me with numerous challenges, most in my self-worth and self-esteem, underscoring my persistent need to be validated; that I am good enough, smart enough and worthy enough; that I am not an extra, not a spare, not a replacement. It is for these reasons that I have always pushed myself, sometimes, beyond what is necessary, in a constant state of substantiating my existence. It is also the reason I have sought confirmation from others, often from those who were limited in their praise and validation. Today, though, I am learning to praise myself and to provide myself with what I need.

Ironically, what saved my marriage, and myself, in indescribable ways, was what I mourned over for years—living hundreds of miles from my mother. I was forced to depend on myself and on Paul in making decisions for our family with limited outside management or interference. Living far from my mother helped me to focus on my own life. Living at opposite ends of the state shielded me from the creation of further mantras, from more pointed criticism, and from even more extreme self-denial.

However, at the same time, I often resented Paul's self-assuredness, which was a constant reminder of the lack of my own. He was confident in his intelligence; he questioned those in authority; and he never hesitated to ask for clarification from anyone. I wrongly believed that his opinions and his directives were primarily to control me and I rebelled in the form of arguments and tantrums. Yet, what I couldn't safely articulate in conversations with my mother, I learned to openly share with Paul. I angrily told him not to tell me what to do, but because of Paul's unconditional love, he was a safe person with whom to share my fury and frustrations, so eventually, I had my own opinions and I safely used them during these exchanges.

Paul created a trusting environment for my disagreements; he never slammed a door, pushing me out; he never left; and he never isolated me. He only came back for more through the eyes of his pure, absolute devotion. He taught me that I could be furious at him and within minutes, return to contentment after an argument or a heated conversation. Our disagreements and arguments didn't last long and there were no harbored resentments that morphed into cruel, pointed remarks to which I had become accustomed in interactions with my mother.

But for years, I still had so much to prove to myself. As a young wife and mother, I was determined to do everything better than others—the best. My cakes were from scratch; my recipes intricately layered with ingredients from multiple trips to various markets; my friendships marked by what I could do for others, never wanting reciprocation. With limited physical and emotional support, I made gourmet dinners while working full time and raising three boys. My friends' approving remarks and encouraging comments, couched in amazement, propelled me further into a whirling dervish of energy and exhaustion, always with an eye on the prize of self-acceptance, but always falling short.

I had to change this dangerous routine, to slow my motor,

and reassure myself against my dreaded fear that I would end up lying in bed for most of my days. I could not continue to keep this pace in my mothering, working, and taking care of the house, not to mention attempting to be a loving partner—all with minimal help. It was my goal to be all things to all people—except to myself. I had torn myself into fragments and there were days that I navigated with fear and bewilderment sometimes actually, in the mornings, counting the 16 hours until I could sleep again.

I read whatever I could on spirituality, on past lives, on inward journeys to wholeness. These writings helped me to understand myself, yet I lacked any form of sustained contentment. My pieces were scrambled and I needed order for my chaos. I returned to weekly therapy and the long process of further examination of my role in my own life and how to put myself back together. For me, talking about the difficult issues that I had suppressed for so long allowed me to become present in my own life and to finally appreciate myself. Despite the slow breakthroughs in coming into my own, I continued to live several lives at once, or so it seemed. I lived for my children, for my husband, my students, while still completely devoted to my mother 400 miles away.

In my early motherhood years, I felt especially sorry for myself for not having my own mother nearby. My friends' mothers babysat and brought in food to help out, in sickness and in health. They came over to their daughters' homes during the day to ease the craziness of the long afternoons of sleepless toddlers. Their moms stayed with the new babies while my friends picked up their older children or ran errands or decadently, got a haircut. They provided weekend reprieves by babysitting so my friends and their spouses could go to a movie and return to a quiet home and sleep in late on Sunday mornings. Some of my friends and their spouses even went on week long vacations, knowing their children were lovingly and willingly taken care of by their respective grandparents. I had none of this help. Even my mother-in-law frequently reminded me of my maternal imperfections and the mistakes I continued to make in raising my boys. The one time she stayed with two of the three boys (before the third was born), for our two nights away, upon our return, she sharply stated in reference to her grandchildren, ages four and a half and two:

"I would rather have another hysterectomy than to ever stay with them again."

I learned not to ask her for help where there was none to give.

Yet, I falsely believed that if I had lived near my own mother, I would have had her support in all areas of my life, especially parenthood. Yet, of course I knew I was fooling myself. I had created a "Kodak moment" of mental images showcasing my adoring mother lovingly playing on the floor with her grandchildren while I calmly walked out the door, hearing her happily remark, *Take your time; no need to rush back.* To believe that my mother's physical and emotional support could exist in helping me with my own children was truly incredulous, as if longing for such a reality made it so.

In all fairness, though, Mother never presented herself as the babysitting-type of grandmother, but when money was tight, she generously offered to send me a monthly check to cover a once-a-week babysitter. What my mother couldn't give in emotional and physical support, she was able to give financially. Every Thursday morning, I left one or two of my sons who weren't in school yet to do whatever I wanted. Mother understood the importance of taking care of herself, yet I fell to the other extreme, doing my best to ignore my own needs as if self-denial and martyrdom were my badges of pride. I wrongly equated self-care with being selfish—a legacy of my mother's mantra about mothers of sons. Despite my hesitations, I still left the house for these four hours, but as I shut the front door, I could never completely remove my feelings of guilt—for leaving my boys with a babysitter; for having a few hours to myself; for anything and everything.

While I slowly became more self-assured in my life without my mother nearby, I also excitedly lived for my parents' biannual visits. Again, Paul reminded me each time how I emotionally regressed when they were present. Such regressions were never pretty and most of the time, Paul lovingly left me to pick up the pieces of myself once they had left. I cried as they drove away, but within minutes, I had begun to live more fully once again, yet I did not give Paul the satisfaction of his incredibly accurate observations.

Both of my parents enjoyed these trips, especially to be with their grandchildren. My father also focused a lot on my life and my teaching, asking me countless questions about what I was doing and thinking. When he could, he would accompany me to work, sit in my classroom, watch me teach, and speak to my students. He adored playing with the boys, swimming with them, going to the market with me, anything that meant togetherness and to make my life a little easier. My mother loved her time with her three grandsons and we also managed to have time together, the two of us, often shopping and having lunch. She wasn't happy that I was working and would frequently say as much, especially if I had to work when they were visiting. I said nothing, unable to defend my life choices of wanting children and wanting a career.

In between my parents' visits to Los Angeles, most all of our family vacations were to San Francisco until the boys' schedules did not coincide with our trips home. In my 40s, almost monthly, I started flying alone to San Francisco to spend time with my parents, but especially to see my father, whose debilitating stroke took his gait and his language during the last eight years of his life. We both looked forward to our time together, playing dominoes at the kitchen table every afternoon at 4:00 with our respective glasses of Chardonnay.

I made these visits home a priority despite my work schedule and the needs of my husband and sons. My schedule didn't matter—only what I could do for my father once I was there. I would fly in on a Thursday after work and leave on a Sunday morning. My mother, though, had her own way of processing my time spent with them:

"We can't count Thursday and Sunday is out, so you are really only here 1½ days."

How my mother cut almost four days down to one and a half days I will never know, but her words underscored the message that no matter how much time I spent with her, she felt it was never enough. I didn't argue with her or plaintively explain the physical and emotional hardship in taking this time away from my life as wife, mother, and professor; she would not understand.

Yet, my mother was justifiably frightened and angry— having to make sure my father was well taken care of, running the house, and having a routine she resented at this stage of her life.

I wanted to help her, but I knew I couldn't. She wanted her house to herself, yet suddenly my father became an invalid and required a 24/7 caretaker along with my mother's constant support for the man who had always taken care of her. Because I was so close to her and so safe, she lashed out at me, especially knowing that I could leave and return to my own life far from hers.

"Do you know how hard it is? I have to market, plan meals, cook for three of us every day. This isn't what I bargained for, that's for sure. Life isn't fair. Poor Daddy. Look at my life now."

To validate her legitimate despair, I responded: "I'm sorry. I know it's so hard."

Mom replied, "No, you really don't know how hard it is. You're not here."

Most of her comments punctuated by frustration at her situation ended with the same words to me: *You're not here.* Silence was always my response to a statement of fact that was also laced with her anger and loss.

During these visits, my father, his caretaker, and I would take daily walks or drive to the San Francisco Zoo, one of his favorite places, while most of the time, my mother stayed home. The stroke had aged my father almost overnight, from a chubby, energetic man, to one that filled his wheelchair with his frail, thin body, always covered with a blanket for warmth. Yet, my father's simple pleasures showed me another way to live stoically and humbly and happily. Even without his ability to talk, when I looked into his eyes, I never fell short; I never saw loss; I saw gratitude, pride, and complete adoration.

When I returned home from these frequent visits, I once again immersed myself into my full life, far away from a miserably sad mother and an ailing father. However, an underpinning of guilt was never far from the surface, gnawing at me as I replayed my mother's words: *You're not here.*

My increasing introspection through my education, my readings and my therapy allowed me to see that for most of my life, I looked to others for affirmation, consolation, and confidence, assured that they would provide what I lacked. Even Paul, while wonderful in countless ways, never uttered the exact words I longed to hear:

You are an amazing mother. You have done so well with the boys. You are the best wife I could ever have.

Granted, he purchased greeting cards with such sentiments, so I knew of his true feelings, but I needed to hear them while forcing myself to feel and internalize them. While healthier souls just accept the truth without another having to say the words, a second-best child often needs these words to be spoken. It has been a long process to accept for years what I had sought through external validation. Today I provide my own words of support, often talking to myself:

You have done a great job in your marriage, Barbara. You have stayed together four decades when there were times it would have been easy to walk away, to let go. The same for motherhood. It was a challenge to raise your three boys, at times dealing with many serious issues, yet you did the best you could, which is all anyone ever can do. You were the best daughter you could be, often unappreciated by the very woman to whom you devoted your life.

Sadly, the ultimate test of my internal growth came at the end of my mother's life. Although neither one of us knew it would be the last time we would see each other, just two weeks before my mother died, we were lying together on her bed—she under the sheets and I, on top. The television was on, yet we weren't watching. My mother held her book, yet she wasn't reading.

She quietly stated what she must have been pondering:

"Someone must have put an evil eye on me. Look at me."

Despite the fact that she could go and come with the aid of a helper, had enough money for her needs and wants, lived in the same house for 52 years, I assumed Mother was referring to not feeling well; not being able to do what she once did. She felt victimized; someone or something had cast a spell on her and placed her in this limiting physical position—not the 85 birthdays she had celebrated. I never knew what to say after such statements. I didn't want to respond the way she would have responded to me, with an invalidating retort:

You should be thrilled to have arrived at old age with your mind intact. You have had such a great life with a husband who adored you, two devoted, productive kids, five grandchildren and two great-grandchildren—all the while never having to work a day in your life. What are you thinking?

No, I learned the importance of supporting one's feelings through the lack of such support of my own. Instead, I responded with acknowledgment of her challenges:

"I know it's hard, but you're doing so well."

"No," she added, "Not really. What was my life really for? What did I really do? You have your own life and I'm here. You don't need me."

I suddenly understood the direction of our conversation and that her end-of-life recount would not include a gratitude list. Without warning, the focus of her reflective monologue had shifted to me, to what I hadn't given her in her lifetime, which was a daughter living near her, one to take care of her. Regrettably, it took me decades to accept that absolutely nothing I did, nothing I said, and nothing I felt really mattered to my mother. I broke the one crucial rule—I left The City of my birth, I left her, and she punished me for most of my life for this act—the very act that paradoxically saved my own soul.

But I didn't talk to her about my decision to permanently stay in Los Angeles or having left her to begin my own life. Instead, I told her what was almost impossible to say and what I didn't believe but voiced anyway:

"I'm sorry that I wasn't the daughter you wanted me to be."

Even at this late date in my own life, I actually believed that my astute response would fully vindicate me from a lifetime of never quite measuring up. I imagined her stating that not only was I the daughter she wanted me to be, but that I was the best daughter in the world, that she was so happy to have had me after such a traumatic loss. Her only comment stunned me:

"We don't always get what we want."

I responded in silence, yet I heard an ever-so-slight "snap" from within my soul. The tentative little girl who sought

validation from her mother was slowly yet finally replaced
by a more self-assured woman who knew she was the best of
daughters.

Had our final exchange occurred earlier in my own life,
when my self-esteem and heartstrings were anchored to my
mother's words, I would have been destroyed, a puddle on the
floor to be absorbed. So how could I literally detach from such
painful, limiting words... from the very person I was so devoted
to yet who had the power to wound me with one raised eyebrow,
one smirk, or her emphasis on the vowels as she called out my
name? Quite frankly, it has taken me years, decades, to come
into my own.

Since that conversation, the painful fragments of memory
have dulled, and I have learned to give myself a break in the areas
of my life where serenity had previously eluded me. I do my best
to ignore the now-silenced internalized maternal voice reminding
me of where I have fallen short, landing just off the mark.

It has been my glorious yet painful journey that, despite
the limiting beliefs I grew to own, I was also able to slowly—
very slowly, let go, allowing them to flutter away, pushed away by
a slowly rediscovered inner strength. Today, through the glory of
acceptance I tell myself... *Yes, Barbara, you were the best daughter
you could be, especially under turbulent circumstances.*

I recognize how I grew into adulthood and motherhood
with emotional braces and I remember again, how strong I
have become so that I can let such limitations fall away. And, I
gratefully remember the light-hearted, hysterically funny woman
my mother could be, the woman I loved unconditionally.

Chapter Seven
Reflections on My Inward Journey

The uplift of a fearless heart will help us over other sorts of barriers. —Laura Ingalls Wilder

Reflections on Food

I am well into middle age despite being told that 60 is the new 50, which I don't quite believe, for the mirror recognizes my weathered storms that have left their permanent imprint within the lines on my face and the gray through my color-treated hair. I am the age that I am and I am a survivor of sorts, the replacement child.

Today, I am a works-in-progress toward wholeness, diligently strengthening my self-confidence and self-esteem. I own these weaknesses despite acknowledging their origins. Early on, a fragile self-worth molded me into the young child who could fit wherever I was needed into my family of origin, a little girl who spent her years pleasing at the expense of herself. These limitations created the adult who became the 'yes' girl; the people pleaser; the easy-going harmonizer for almost any situation. Today, such qualities constrict opportunities for healthy boundaries and become a target for those who want to take advantage of my agreeable nature.

I am constantly working on developing a healthier dose of self-assurance in my relationships with family, friends, colleagues.

Others do not sense the emotional volleyball match within, but as the replacement-child, this is my challenging legacy. My young adult feelings of inadequacy were initially punctuated by not feeling smart enough, thin enough, hard-working enough, and good enough at almost everything, eventually, molding me into an adult version of believing that I was not a good-enough wife, mother, and, of course, most of all, daughter.

My introspection, the examination of my fragility, has ultimately provided me the strength to live more boldly today. My soul knew what I hadn't yet articulated—that I needed to completely accept my understudy legacy in order to live more fully for the rest of my days. Regardless of the circumstances, my reclaimed inheritance is to live outside the shadow of a little boy's incomplete life and to view myself as an original instead of a substitute. I can exist fully, owning my passions, my desires, my needs, and equally, my dislikes. Even more, I can verbalize my feelings—all of them, whether others agree or choose to listen, for I am listening—yes, I am finally listening to my own voice and I hear:

You have been enough; you have always been enough!

I very much believe that my mother did the best she could with her children, as I have done with my own. Mother loved me when she could, but there were times when she was so emotionally spent that all she could do was to listlessly drag herself into bed, leaving me to turn inward, to the pages of the novels and memoirs I adored and the daily pages of my own writing. Today, I accept that my intense love for my mother was not reciprocated in a language that I understood—in words or hugs or open doors.

It was my mother's own mother, my Nana Bea, who emotionally and physically nurtured me throughout my childhood while also caring for her internally tormented daughter. Most days, Nana Bea greeted me at the door upon my return from school, gave me my snack, and in the afternoons, sat with my mother in the golden goose down armchair next to her bed. My grandmother's sweet, even temperament balanced my mother's bouts of hysteria, providing a calm connection to my young life. Receiving unconditional love from even one parent and grandparents enables a child to grow up with workable issues, issues that can eventually be fixed with time and reflection. I gratefully learned this along the way.

While I have come to accept my anxious mothered and mothering lives, I alone take responsibility for an eating disorder that I have sadly nurtured and ironically fed my entire life. Although now I am thin—or so I am told, it is a challenging concept for me to own and I acknowledge such irrational thoughts. However, I am often confused when every once in a while, a friend or acquaintance will remark that I must have lost weight. Actually, it isn't the weight that people notice, as the scale has stayed virtually the same in the past three decades. It is because I still find odd comfort in wearing clothing that is too big for me, pointed out to me while in a department store browsing at a rack of clothing.

The sales associate asked me my size and I responded with the size I was currently wearing and the one that filled my closet—"8."

"Oh, no," she responded with assertiveness. "You must be a 4."

I literally laughed aloud, but at that moment, I also had a glimpse of clarity. Could it be that I actually saw myself at least two sizes larger than perhaps another person viewed me? I finally succumbed to this 20-something sales associate who pleaded with me to at least try on something in my actual size— the one that my young high school girlfriends would have worn so long ago—the impossibly unattainable number I had envied so much. At that same moment as her comment, I also heard my mother's voice reverberate within, *Don't let the material cup your bottom.* Yet, I grabbed the tinier size and ran with it, almost fearful to try the pants on again at home. I instantly removed the tags so I could not return them, still unable to honestly discern the image in front of me—my image.

Wearing clothing that truly fits requires an emotional adjustment. I am used to the comfort and the protection of folds, material with pleats, even when the current styles do not have pleats, and shirts whose buttons have never stretched, button-down shirts that become my 'pullovers.' I cannot judge whether the clothing fits well, for my decision-making in this area is still impaired and I irrationally assume that everything makes me look chunky.

Often times, I use self-talk, telling myself that the pants look good despite feeling that I am poured into them. Little by little, today, I am allowing myself the gift of actually searching the clothing racks in my size—not in a size to be grown into or so roomy that I disappear; I am letting myself exist physically, to be seen through my clothing instead of protected by excess material.

Eating disorders are insidious and I am thankful that I was able to come back from the abyss of permanent physical disaster, yet this challenge for me still remains. At first a way to lose weight, to fit into the tiny clothes that my best friend Lori could slide into, slowly evolved into my chosen method of control and a way for my mother to acknowledge my existence. Yet, after decades of living with my starvation secret and self-inflicted restrictions, I can more freely address my food issues with less uncomfortable silence. As with any limitation, I am learning to celebrate the moments of normalcy and to replace my internal voice of deprivation with affirmations of abundance and acceptance.

While many of my family and friends believe my meal choices are all just a result of my health consciousness, I acknowledge that my eating is far too erratic and limited, and at times, peculiar, to be considered wholesome. Many of my food selections are based on scarcity instead of satiation. I choose hunger pains, strangely comforting pangs from long ago when self-denial always won over self-nurturing. My irrational fear of the scale continues, whether at home or at the doctor's office.

At my age, I should eat what I want and when I want, but still, sadly, I take daily inventory of my food intake. Effective deprivation enables me to awake the following morning knowing that the previous day's limitations have maintained my slimness, which oddly I still cannot own in my reflection. If, on the other hand, I eat too much of one item, my food monitoring on the following day requires extra vigilance, further self-punishment.

While I now understand the origins of my eating issues, I am left to pick up the pieces at this late stage without knowing how they quite fit together. Within this journey, I have lost both my physical and emotional compass, traded, initially, for a pair of skinny jeans. Long past the trendy, coveted garb, today, I am an older woman coming to terms with the demons that fill my thoughts about food, but really about myself.

Depriving myself, starving myself, were the ways in which I could control the uncontrollable—my mother's strong rule over my young, hesitant life. She could tell me what to wear, deprive me of owning a pair of beloved jeans, and instruct me who to date and when to marry him, but she could not force me to chew and to swallow. While it is helpful to look back in order to see the 'whys' of my actions of today, living in the past only removes my own responsibility for an enriched life, free of such constraints. Only I can extricate myself from the limiting beliefs and chains of my self-inflicted deprivations regardless of how and when they began.

While I have learned to nourish my soul and feed my emotional needs, eating the foods that can pleasurably sustain my body remains an enormous challenge despite understanding such irrational dynamics. I have gotten so adept at focusing on what I must have to continue my cycle of deprivation, that I sadly discount my own taste buds and desires. I actually walk through an entire buffet line, filled with international food stations, oozing with creamy cheese laden pastas, slippery golden noodles, five cuts of juicy, red beef, chunky pieces of bright yellow, shinny and gooey macaroni n' cheese, yet I allow myself only visions of the salad bar's fresh vegetables and fruit platters, perhaps croutons, if it has been a profitable day of scarcity. I view the other customers laughing, gulping and swallowing, returning to the buffet line, socializing through food, not worrying what eating so much means for them at their next meal, and, once again, I am in my own private hell.

I often walk through food courts and out of the corner of my eye, I view a young, full-figured woman inhaling her overflowing fork of glistening Chow Mein noodles and her readiness to pierce the pile of orange chicken on her plate. I watch with my own suppressed cravings, an older, round man, as he blissfully stuffs his mouth with his high-caloric pizza, laden-filled with pepperoni and cheese and deliciousness. I want to be this woman and this man, so comfortable in their eating and talking, seemingly disinterested about any additional pounds that might register on tomorrow's scale. Yet, I continue to longingly examine a menu and then order what I feel I should have from the "light and healthy" section, not even knowing what else the restaurant offers to "normal" people who actually eat what they desire.

My withdrawal from food that is deliciously comforting and satisfying digs deep and has affected how I view the world. It has become 'them'—the natural eaters and enjoyers— and 'me.' The 'me' is lonely, alone, starving, unable to consistently partake in the emotional and physical pleasure of eating that others duly accept as their God-given right—the right to consume good food and enjoy, whether it is a bag of potato chips or a hot dog. I have gotten this good—and this bad. I have this much self-control—a self-control that has slowly killed my joy of eating.

I ask myself, If not now, when? I tell myself I am entitled to taste delicious, calorie-ridden food, especially because I do not abuse the privilege, that I will not go down the road of eating myself into oblivion as I once did during my chubby days, yet this was easily over 40 years ago. I still don't trust that I will maintain my weight even after decades of doing so or by my reflection in the mirror.

Yes, I have become a professional in knowing when to stop; today, though, my problem is that, sadly, I do not know when to start. I still suffer silently, but I have not given up trying to conquer my eating disorder that has controlled me for most of my life.

Reflections on Friendships

As I grew into womanhood I now know that I did not do anything wrong, that I was not defective in my feelings and sharing such emotions with my mother. As I grew into womanhood, without awareness of my search, I discovered support and solace from other mother-type women, but never my own mother; I came to understand that her well was dry long before I needed her—before I was born. I have slowly learned the worthiness of my emotions and the importance of acknowledging all of them, at the same time recognizing the personal loss in the inability to share them with the one woman who I sought comfort.

The depth of my introspection has driven me far inward, with much of my time spent intensely exploring my own life with limited involvement in the mundane areas of others' lives. It is not comfortable for many to converse on such an in-depth level of reflection, but for me it's hard to resurface, to make small talk after having painstakingly considered the big-ticket items of my life. By my own doing, I spend more time alone, yet at the same time, I am more comfortable in my own skin, enjoying the pockets of solitude that my mind offers, all gifts of gradual self-acceptance.

Yet, many other women may not be too comfortable around me when they sense that I burrow so deeply into myself. At times I do not come up for air, which is far too heavy for a light lunch date with a friend who doesn't quite understand where I have gone. Instead, I seek other women, like myself, who work so hard on their internal journeys—who acknowledge their difficulties and together discuss solutions. This is where I am most comfortable—down deep where the veiled shadows often obscure my vision and where the light flickers in hope.

Lori's friendship is the most enduring, lasting our entire lives, yet we have never lived in the same city and our families have never comingled as often happens with women—sharing babysitting, carpools, and family celebrations. Yet, our 60-plus years of friendship also includes a relevant modern connection binding us beyond just our shared family history. It is a friendship of our hearts, sharing emails, readings, and annual get-aways, where we reconnect to a linked past with parents who were best friends. I never have to explain myself to Lori, who with words of tender comfort will often say to me, "I get it, pal." She surely does.

I have several other dear friends—women who are there for me as I am for them. I have always needed and will continue to need these special girlfriends in my life. Marilyn falls under the category of best friend and sister, and with her, I can open my heart and together we examine the pieces of joy and sadness. She was the best daughter-in-law any mother of a son could hope to have, and my mother knew it. Stephen brought her into my life when I was 14 and she immediately melted into the fabric of my being. She is the only other female, besides my mother, who has reminded me to take a sweater on a chilly evening.

This counts for everything.

Reflections on Marriage

Within my journey to wholeness, I acknowledge my marriage, which has endured four decades. We have come together in a healthy affection, one contingent on trust and mutual reverence. I am grateful for these lessons, for the unconditional love that Paul has shown me, and even more, taught me to feel, so that I could raise our children with such a gift, one that was given to me by my father and grandmother as well. Life was often challenging for us and there were times I wanted to flee from him, from us, from our children. When times were intolerable, I blamed Paul for what wasn't his fault, but he was the safest person to attack. We mainly argued over parenting, which was so ironic to me. We started a family based on our love and the very elements that created such a family were the ones that pulled us a part. But we endured. We endured because of our tenaciousness, our love, and guidance from others.

I needed validation that didn't come from Paul, so I sought therapy. I expected Paul to fix what was broken within me—an impossible task for another. I lost my defensiveness and my ego. It didn't matter who was right. Did I want to be right or at peace? I chose the latter and it has made all the difference. He is a good man—perhaps one of the best. We have both changed within our marriage, but his devotion to me has never wavered. He has continually put me first in his life even when he was not first in my life. We have come through the dark tunnel of childhood illnesses and teenage years together and now we are enjoying a level of serenity that we never had, a wordless understanding of our togetherness. I am so grateful for Paul's ability to let me be me, something my mother never was able to do.

Reflections on My Career

Today, I continue to teach my college students, whom I adore, how to write effectively for their academic courses. I am devoted to their progress and feel honored to instruct them. I have come into my own as an educator and understand that while I want my students to be successful, I cannot want it more than they want it. I have learned to let go and let them be responsible for their choices, just as I was with my own. It is a sense of freedom to understand that some may have to fail in order to eventually succeed. I am there when they falter, but I also know I cannot pick them up without their desire.

I am untroubled in my excommunication by the college's administration; I only care a tiny bit that I am not liked by unlikable people. To deny this would be dishonest. But their displeasure in me does not send me into a panic as in the past. I accept that not everyone likes me and with great relief, I also finally accept that I don't have to like everyone. What a simple but incredibly difficult lesson for me to learn. Limiting my people pleasing ways has freed me to be present in my own life.

I can actually spend this same energy on making myself happy.

Reflections on Motherhood

Being the mother of adult sons, for me, has been a tremendous, continuous challenge. My maternal instincts do not turn off merely because they are now men on their own, men with their own lives, and men with their own loves. I want to speak to them daily, to know what they are feeling and thinking and doing. Yet, I appreciate that these are my desires and not theirs; today and I have learned to honor their needs while also acknowledging my own. So, this is what I do. I read more; I write; and I focus on myself; and what I want to accomplish in the final years of my life. I am learning to let go; to be content within my own skin; to stop searching and seeking, to be.

No life partner, no children, no best friend, and no job can provide me with the gifts I have uncovered—the self-love to live my life peacefully. I adored my mother perhaps more than any other human being in this world. I gave her my heart with open hands, for her to mold in the way she could. This was too much for her to accept and I know she did what she could. Yet, it is up to me to remold my heart in a way that gives me joy and reminds me of my inner beauty, which no one can alter. All my life I have willingly given away pieces of myself, first to my mother, then to my husband and children, and to my supervisors at work. I never knew I didn't have to do this, that I could keep the part of me that belonged just to me and share tiny fragments…on loan…to borrow. I also cannot hope that someone who loves me will know exactly what I am thinking or what I need to make my life complete. Only I can provide what I need in this way.

I have always felt as if I have lived two lives at once, running faster, sometimes from myself, staying far away from a bed even when I needed such respite. Part of my push to do more is the result of my position as the replacement child, trying to justify my existence to my mother, to show her in countless ways that I was not just a result of her acquiescence in accepting another pregnancy, but that I rightfully belonged in this world, and to her.

I have also feared being idle, terrified that my gifts of a zest and energy for life would be unused, like my mother's. I was so fearful of assuming her darkness, of giving up to a down comforter and a pillow that I refused to sit still even when such rest was warranted, when it is still warranted. However, the other part of this frenetic push to do more and be more, seeking my completeness, is actually a gift from the child who never grew up. Jeffrey, whose spirit has been with me every step of the way, guiding me in my writing and in my life, revealing my intense, internal journey.

I ponder my joy of shopping, wondering why I obtain so much pleasure from the physical act of walking around a store—it doesn't even matter which store, what department, even what I buy or if I buy. I only have to focus my mind's eye on our threesome—my mother, grandmother, and I, together shopping, in this pecking order, with my mother, upset or pleased, depending on what we found to successfully fit my roundness, depending on how many colors in which we found the same pair of pants.

Even today, it is this connectedness, this closeness for which I long whenever I enter any store. It is not the act of purchasing, but the act of searching, breathing in the perfumed scents, strolling, joining arms; even when my mother pulled away, there was always the potential for closeness this time, the chance to make her happy in finding something to fit me. Department stores were the one place in which my mother and I could walk together, parallel, without the need to make eye contact, yet we were in sync in our day's mission. Once I shared with a therapist that my only consistent positive memories with my mother were of shopping.

His comment has stayed with me forever, "At least you had shopping."

Yes, at least I had shopping.

Today when I feel the loss of my mother, I only have to return to the stores she frequented to feel at one with her. After she died it took me almost a full year before I could return to her almost-daily eatery—a café in one of the large department stores. Despite the location being in a different city, until their recent renovations, the restaurants were laid out in the exact ways—down to every table, chair and spoon. This sameness reassured me and deeply saddened me.

While I acknowledge that many children are born under far worse conditions, a necessary part of my growth and my peace has come through the reflection of my life-long experiences, often framed and viewed through my own lens as the runner-up. I have always sensed that for me to have an enriched life, I needed to examine the jagged fragments of my soul, whose pieces when pressed together, do not quite match, yet in almost fitting, they suffice.

I understand so much more now—why I am such a people pleaser; why I have spent countless years worrying about what others think; and why sadly, I have cared about others' wishes and feelings at the expense of my own. Such reflections of my beginnings have given me the gift of self-understanding—why I continually strive to be better than enough, even when I do not have to try so hard anymore in any area of my life. I have finally learned to turn up the volume of my own voice, to shout out my needs, my own dreams and hopes, recognizing that it's not too late to demand to be first. None of these revelations come easily for me; it continues to be a daily struggle, but one that I am finally winning.

I pushed relentlessly against forces both in my control and those I could not foresee. At times, I have literally felt as if I were swimming upstream in clouded water, navigating by my heart only, which, when I follow, has always pointed me in the right direction. Today, I refuse to see myself as runner up in my own life and, gloriously, I have nothing more to prove to anyone. I can wait no longer, so I am now the voice I need to hear. I create my own mantra of affirmation even if it is a challenge to own and embrace such positive words. I am determined to live completely.

My introspection has helped me to search for the beginning of the rope drifting in the waters where my journey began, pulling toward it, strengthening and righting my present course. Some say that we can 'look back,' but we should not 'stare,' and I think this is fine advice. I would not want to rewrite any part of my life's script...only to fine-tune my todays so that the unfinished scenes will reflect a more fully serene and glorious journey.

Today, my loose ends can be neatly tucked away in a presentable fashion. I am softer with myself, understanding that we all walk with something. One day, far in the future, when I am no longer here, I hope to be remembered for trying...for trying in so many areas of my life, for tirelessly working for what I wanted—the personal life roles I so adored—daughter, wife, and mother, yet in which I feared coming up short, in which I felt I was not enough.

Perhaps one can say I overcompensated, I worked too hard when adequacy would have sufficed. I would agree, but I never knew I didn't have to trudge through the darkness in my path; quite simply, my internal gage was broken and I let my fears guide and define me. In my decades-long process toward self-acceptance, while I might have disappointed those I loved, I never did so intentionally. With humility, the only person I have short-changed in this intimate journey has been myself, struggling to accept myself as I was and am, my legacy of having replaced a sweet baby boy who never got to grow up.

Jeffrey, a little boy whom I never knew, and who was not talked about, became one of the most important people in my life. Although Stephen was completing kindergarten when Jeffrey died, the little brother who was dressed like him and whose hand he held in faded sepia photos, left no imprint on our older brother. For Stephen, it is as if his little brother never existed. Ironically, while I could have never known Jeffrey, I feel as if I have known him quite well, all of my life. This book, which began as an introspective tool to help me put the pieces of my life back together, is also a tribute to a little life that never got to grow up, a little boy whose main destiny, ironically, was to provide space for his sister to exist.

Chapter Eight
Acceptance and Gratitude

I read and walked for miles at night along the beach, writing bad blank verse and searching endlessly for someone wonderful who would step out of the darkness and change my life. It never crossed my mind that that person could be me. —Anna Quindlen

I have countless gifts in my life today, most the result of my continuous introspection and my relentless determination to uncover the layers that come together to create my soul's brilliant design. Actually, my replacement child legacy has become one of these gifts, for I have learned my ultimate lessons through uncovering my fragile beginnings. While I arrived because another departed, I was meant to be here and my lifetime journey to discover and accept my distinctive spirit has resulted in the beauty unfolding daily.

I have had many challenges, some that have brought me to my knees, forced me to scream and cry and question, yet I have never faltered in the realization that there are glorious lessons to be learned in all of these experiences, from the joys and from the burdens. I am learning to accept all the parts of me, grateful for their blend into my unique magnificence. I accept the reality of my mother's qualified love for me, surging in intermittent waves; I also blissfully accept my own capacity to love her unconditionally. These recognitions are all amazing rewards of my inward journey.

Despite our shared challenges, I know my mother loved me, and I feel confident that she knew I loved her. Most all of our phone calls ended with telling my mother just this, and sometimes she would respond with "Love you." Early on in my quest for answers, for wholeness, I would, with dejected offence, analyze her retort, noticing she never uttered "I" before her words of endearment, not quite understanding that, perhaps, the inclusion of the personal pronoun for her was too exposing, too revealing. However, a gift of my search and my contemplations has been acceptance. What my mother was able to give, I accept and what she couldn't, I accept this, too... today.

Although I filtered most of our phone calls in order to elicit her gentle responses, it saddens me that these conversations are gone forever even if meals, clothing, and weather were the focus of such benign calls. I am grateful for the 54 years we shared as mother and daughter. Clearly, while I grew into my adult life with huge deficits, I do not hold her or any other person accountable; I only acknowledge their beginnings in order to change my course, for this is my responsibility.

Through the seemingly endless layers of my inward search, I have learned that because of the mother I had, I get to be the mother I wanted. I am loving, giving and generous of spirit with my sons. I tell my boys that I love them no matter what they do or do not do; no matter what they say or do not say; no matter whether they agree or disagree. I do not make threats or take away my love, even when they hurt me. I have always told them that they can be whatever they want because it is true. I tell them that I know they will make the best decisions for themselves despite my silent fears. I accept their lives are separate from my own. I also accept none of this is easy.

Once my mother told me that she regretted giving me some of her jewelry because she never saw me wear the pieces even though I treasured these generational heirlooms and wore the rings and bracelets on special occasions when she wasn't with me. So, I get to give freely without strings attached and do not expect accountability for gifts long gone. I also accept that when upsetting events happen to me, it's not due to an evil eye; it's just what happens in life. And, finally, I can admit that I still miss my mother horribly but feel profound relief from her daily dose of disappointment reflected in her tone, remarks, and pointed silence. When I was younger, such disgust and disapproval were reflected in closed doors, yet today I keep my doors open.

I assume that if my mother were alive to read this book, she would defensively qualify her actions, refuse to ask questions or even speak to me. She would be dismayed by my reflections and revelations; threaten to change her Will as she had so often, and would inform me of my irrational views of my very fortunate childhood and young adulthood. There would be retribution in her silence, in her sudden, discontinued phone calls. Most likely she would remind me that I had nothing to complain about after all she had done for me and that I was lucky to have ever been born. I hear echoes of these anticipated remarks, but today, I can tenderly, yet fervently respond, *Yes, you did so much for me, and, yes, I was lucky to be born, but I have every right to inscribe my truth, for it is mine.*

It has taken me a lifetime to find the comfort in self-validation and to accept the truth that remains not in absolutes, not in black or white thinking, but in the gray, undefined areas. I can share my reality about a distraught, unraveling mother who loved fiercely, yet intermittently, and, who at times, could also be my confidant, guiding me with unequivocal honesty and affection.

My painful, extraordinary insights are translated through my own perspective of remembrance, with perhaps another person, such as my older brother Stephen, interpreting the dynamics in quite a different way, yet this is my vision, my truth, and my reality.

Through my interactions with my mother, I learned that I could not safely share with her many of my feelings or my differences of opinion. Yet, today I finally possess a profound comfort in sharing my emotions whether or not they are reciprocated or validated by others, for I proudly and humbly own them.

As I aged, I also recognized my endless submissions provided few benefits. A perennial pushover, one who responds in silence, is not endearing, and my growth and maturity depended on verbally protecting and defending myself. At first, awkwardly, I responded with my very raw emotions, all negated through others' logical discussion. Then, I went to the other extreme, yelling and screaming, allowing my increased volume and hysteria to provide my defense. Eventually, though, I came to state my feelings; to disagree with respect; and finally to tolerate this rather messy and uneasy process of owning my voice. I am grateful for this extended lesson of self-approval, which was born from the unsteady foundation of my existence. My younger years forced me to substantiate my presence so frequently that such efforts became part of the fabric of my being. No more. I am free of the burden to justify myself, a gift of this inward passage.

Less than two months before he died, my father and I were sitting at the kitchen table in the midst of our daily afternoon domino game. Suddenly my father stopped playing, and with his only functioning arm, picked up my hand. He stared at me with such intensity that it was impossible to look away. His crystal blue eyes welled up with tears as he kissed my hand; with words he could not articulate, his silence indicated that he knew we would not see each other again. I followed his cue in validation of his message and told him he was the best father anyone could have had and I was honored to be his daughter. I thanked him for so much in my life; for being my role model; for his unconditional love; for doing his best; and then I kissed him. I am grateful that we could say goodbye to each other through this shared poignant, non-verbal discourse between our souls. He died before my next visit home.

My husband and I have been through so much in our lives, with the usual challenges of raising three children and also the unexpected sufferings. We became a family that experienced drug abuse and the reverberations of decisions made to save our son from his downward spiral. We had to send him away in order to make him well, tearing our hearts in two, suffering the silence and culpable guilt that addiction reeks on loved ones. Although buried within the layers of our anguish, we never completely lost sight of the love we had for each other, and, of course, for our children, so we weathered this private storm and we continued. We fell apart, each sibling mourning the loss and detachment and then slowly picking up the pieces of our family once again. Absolute love helped us come together, helped us mend, as did our eventual ability to share blameless and authentic conversations.

We survived and today each has his perspective of memory, especially our son who suffered the painful consequences of his drug abuse. Today, he accepts responsibility for his choices, strengthened by the agonizing life he chose to leave behind. During this mournful, very sad time, when I was so grief-stricken, my mother's infinite patience and concern for her grandson afforded me yet another way in which to view her and love her. She never criticized when she could have and she never blamed when others communicated their judgment of our parenting through their expressions and their silence. Actually, my mother's door was open for me during this time and she reminded me of how I was saving my son's life. She reinforced how essential it was not to ignore problems with children, not to sweep issues under the carpet, and I listened. I will forever be eternally grateful for the way in which she supported me through this dark time.

When I could have easily justified away my son's irrational behavior to his teenage angst, I confronted my fears and his addiction head on. I came face to face with consequences, his and mine. He needed help before prison or death would take him. I, too, needed to address my enabling behavior that only perpetuated his excuses that I so easily justified. Thus, through this tragedy, I learned about myself. In trying to rescue my son through accepting his lies, his inappropriate, dangerous behavior, through giving him second and third chances, I was harming and limiting him despite my good intentions, intentions based on love. I found my voice, the voice used to make an overwhelmingly inconceivable decision to save his life, and I finally grew up; I finally heard myself speak and I acted, all supported by my mother's unwavering concern and care. How grateful I am to her and for my own strength in surviving and ultimately thriving through the blackness of our son's addiction and ultimate recovery.

Another gift of this heartbreaking time in our lives was the realization that what Mother couldn't give to her daughter— infinite patience and unconditional love—she was able to give to all of her grandsons. I felt her love through them and it became almost enough for me. While her tolerance for me was elusive, she always lovingly accepted the boys.

When I would sometimes complain about what they did or didn't do, she responded, "Don't put your head on their shoulders," rightfully reminding me that they were individuals with their own thoughts, separate from my own. She never measured their closeness by how many phone calls her grandsons made or didn't make to her. "Boys don't do that, Barbara," was all she would say and she truly meant it. She knew they cared and thought of her and that was enough for her.

There was dispensation for all of their foibles and she simply accepted what they could give. My boys, then, experienced a grandmother who was far different than the mother about whom I have written. Their grandmother was absolute in her love and affection for them. For this I am grateful.

My lack of confidence, my fear of making mistakes and being an inadequate mother all increased my motherhood challenges. But, with my three sons grown, I can see that in trying to do what I thought was right for them, my best, I did just that. Regardless of my anxieties, they are kindhearted men with keen intellects and senses of humor. Their compassionate ways will enable them to be resilient, loving fathers. I am joyful in that they actually want to spend time with me and tell me as much. My outdated, innermost voice shouts that they really don't mean what they say, but I know they do, for my sons' honesty is profound. While I am not the most significant woman in their lives anymore, I know I am still very important.

Finally, another gift of my introspective travels is that I don't have to be number one in order to trust that I am still loved and appreciated by my boys or anyone. To know they are out in the world vibrantly creating, working, loving, must be enough for me. Each has his unique personality and quirks, reflecting a little of their father and me, but they are their own persons and I honor their confidence in earning a living in areas of their passion, in pursuing their desires, something I did, but with limitations, with emotional constraints, with trepidation. I always told them to follow their bliss, their joys, no matter what. Truthfully, I didn't always trust my own words, but because my comments were essential to their well-being, I expressed them nonetheless. What my mother could not articulate, to advise me to pursue my deepest desires, I have been able to say to my boys and for this I am thankful.

I often see my three sons as fine-tuned versions of their mother, sharper images, less blurry and blended than my own, especially in their self-esteem and self-assurance. They are strong in the areas I am weak. I see them at restaurants ordering the food they savor and the ways in which they expect it to be prepared. They ask for what they want and need, not with an air of superiority but an innate understanding of what they rightfully and unquestionably deserve. They have expectations of themselves, and for the world around them, knowledge I have had to acquire through my painstaking journey of self-discovery. When they ask for what they want and are denied, they do not crumble; they are not defined by another as their mother was.

My sons are still young, but they need vacations from their daily routines and they take them. They have learned to first take care of themselves before another, but not in a selfish way, but in a healthy way that provides them self-care. There is no martyrdom in their schedules, for they work hard and then they play hard. How could they have learned this from me when I never knew how to do this for myself? Were they watching their father who does just this to take care of himself, a healthier soul than I? Perhaps they were. How glorious to see them so emotionally fit, so strong and so understanding of their own needs and desires. I cannot take much credit for their resilient spirits, only that I lacked my own and worked to an extreme not to pass down this legacy. In this sense, perhaps, I have helped them strengthen their inner core because my own was so lacking.

My memories, all of them, actually, when viewed through my mind's misty, nostalgic lens are now treasures, each related to fleeting time. Like a worn, faded photo whose center provides clarity despite the fraying discolored edges, I relive snapshots of my most recent past. It is 3:00 in the afternoon and my parents are napping, my father in what was once my childhood bedroom, for after his stroke, his 24-hour care required a separate, permanent space.

Mother is napping under the sheets and on top of her heating pad in my parents' king-sized bed, which now belongs only to her. Next to her, I am reading in the same golden goose down armchair that my Nana Bea filled every afternoon upon my return from school; the same tufted chair in which my father would envelop himself after a long day at the shirt factory; the same welcoming chair my brother would fold into during his visits. With smiles and joy, it is also the same chair my boys filled when visiting their Nana from their nearby university.

In this well-worn armchair, the material faded from decades of warm bodies unraveling its weave, I listen to the calming and rhythmic breathing of my elderly parents. The television's insignificant soap opera provides soothing background clatter for those otherwise quiet afternoons when I could have been working in Los Angeles; when I could have been home for my own children and husband; when I could have had time to myself. Instead, I chose to be fully present, to close my own eyes and experience my own peaceful repose, knowing that one day, which sadly is today, I would not have my parents' calming, musical snores enveloping me.

I am forever thankful for the inner voice that reminds me of what needs to be overlooked and what remains essential, the choices between doing and being, when I have gratefully chosen the latter, especially at times that are now gone forever. In the silence of such reflection, my priorities speak to me with love and I listen to my memories with gratitude.

Today, this same inner voice also shows me the clarity of my strengths and good fortune, resulting from my resolute quest for my truth. I overcame a mother whose own limitations could have forever defined me, but the healthy part of me instinctively realized I had to be on my own to grow and flourish—in my education and in my adulthood. I was guided away from my home, to Los Angeles, to study courses that would ultimately provide my gratifying career; to meet an honest, decent and loving man; to have my three sons. My unique path, my journey, appeared to be set in stone even before I understood my direction, yet I continued. I never gave up, for I knew there were answers even before I could articulate the questions.

As I am completing my life's magnificent chain, one link at a time, I am grateful for my health, my family, my vocation, and my writing. I am grateful for the fight within that helps me to examine my once-delicate core, built on the obsolete foundation of countless fears. I made so many choices based on a sense of dread. Yet today, such decision-making does not serve me, for it cannot support my personal growth. I am grateful for the gifts of my introspection that enable me to speak up for myself and to accept I am not second best and that I never actually was.

As the child born in exchange for another, Barbara for Jeffrey, the unsteady ground of my existence resulted in my continuously having to prove my presence in all ways to most all people. Now, I gloriously accept *myself*. I am grateful for all that I am and have, for I recognize it has been relentless, intense work; nothing has come easily.

My rewarding career in education enables me to teach others to own and write their truth, inspiring me and reminding me that at any time we can redefine ourselves throughout our journeys. My own pathway of such meditative writing took me through a long, dark tunnel, but I have come out the other end, to experience extreme gratitude for what I have been given and what has been taken. I have endured and flourished, and joyfully accept my growth, reclaiming my sense of self—my worth, my confidence, my esteem.

My reflective writing has helped me to accept my rightful place within my own existence, something only I can give myself, to know that I am nobody's replacement. I have purposefully opened myself up and these pages have been the process for me to put myself back together, an amazing gift. I have lived honorably and completely despite the huge deficits I carry; I have tried my best to fill in the holes of such inadequacies. I remind myself that I have done my best in all these personal roles—as a daughter, a wife, and a mother, often with few inherited tools.

While I have found great solace in writing about the pieces of my life, the pursuit to write such a book has literally eluded me for decades, for I never knew what form my prose would take. I wrote with countless false starts, elated for the beginnings and deeply disappointed in the abrupt endings after only a few pages, trying to ignore my old Honors English teacher's voice from years ago reminding me that I wasn't a strong enough writer to attend her class. Even my husband, when learning of my intent to write about myself, asked me if I had enough to write about. Again, the nagging inner voice attempted to validate his words.

Maybe he's right. Maybe I don't. I'm not special enough to write about.

As I do with my own students, I reminded myself of the words of American writer and essayist Flannery O'Connor, "Anyone who has survived childhood, has enough information to write a lifetime on."

I knew that I had to explore the elements, the foundation, of my own life. But despite my trepidation, I began to trust my process—the process of sitting down at my computer and writing my truth, which became my story—this story.

Ironically, while my writing has helped me heal, at the same time, it has also created a rebirth of my anguish and insecurities and, in a real sense, I have suffered through pain and loss once again. In my written reflections of reconnecting so closely to my replacement-child roots, I regressed. The words that flowed from my heart onto these pages brought me back to my teenage angst when I couldn't find a bathing suit to cover my folds and I cried hysterically in the fitting room with my grandmother and mother who were looking on in frustration and exhaustion.

I also guardedly relived the times my mother slammed her bedroom door in exasperation, closing me off for what felt like days as she lay in her bed. I experienced, yet again, the powerful influence of a despicably demeaning math teacher and anxious parents, who reinforced my own apprehension of numbers, ultimately guiding my confidence away from one of my passions— the study of medicine. I wondered, too, about Jack's hidden love letters and what would have happened if I had received them all and written to him as he patiently awaited my responses.

I consider how my life would have unfolded without the dread that I owned and carried within me for countless years in the form of fear—the fear of not finding a husband after college graduation; the long ago fear of pursuing a non-traditional female career; the fear of not being a good enough mother; the fear of losing my little boys' love as they became men; and finally, the ceaseless fear of not pleasing my mother. I have had to address these anxieties, which together diminished my self-worth, the best way I have known how. I have revisited the doors that I closed myself so that I could accept my vulnerabilities and understand their origins. I have humbly accepted my humanity, and acknowledged that I am flawed but at the same time perfect in my place in the world, my place.

My writing has always transported me into another world. I pray that it always will. It is my internal compass—an essential component of my equilibrium, an integral indicator of all types of moments that today punctuate the remainder of my journey. I have learned to yell at the tentative inner voice of long ago that occasionally shouts of my mediocre prose, reminding me of a potential non-existent audience. *Who will read what you wrote? Who will care?* Today, I can respond with certainty, I will read my words, for they are mine and they are meaningful. I care.

Today, I own my writing, the craft I have loved with such passion, the constant companion to my little-girl tribulations and joys and my adult adulations and grief. I own my talent that I had denied for so many years, times when I allowed others to define my gift. I stopped writing when their voices became my own until a stronger, healthier affirmation awoke within, reminding me of the significance of my own voice, my writer's voice.

My boys have asked to read this book and so I obliged them, but with trepidation and extreme reluctance. Yet, if I am to break my childhood cycle of secrets and silence, to eliminate my perceived polished image in their eyes, then the time is now. I cannot write about the depth of my angst and refuse to share my revelations with the three who constitute so much of my very essence.

Hypocrisy will never define me, so, with one son at a time, I gave them my words, requiring space between each from their anticipated responses in order to settle my soul. Brian, the youngest, asked first for my pages, and so I provided him with the earlier chapters, affording him a window into another dimension of the maternal women in his life. After he read my words, I felt the need to explain; to justify; to remind him that his grandmother loved him so much, but he needed no further clarification. He never defined his Nana through her limitations or her flaws; he seemed to know there was so much more to her; and he loved her, for her. How grateful I was for this response, realizing that I was the only person who needed reassurance and explanations. But then he asked to read the next chapter, the subject of my own motherhood. My doubts resurfaced. I feared bearing the complexity of my personal maternal essence, something that my own mother could never share with me, revelations that would have provided clarity to her darkness. So, I did what I needed to do for my own growth and acceptance. I gave him the pages to read. He called me, crying, to talk about my words that moved him to these tears that are rarely shed in front of me. I was grateful for his response, for this connection.

I had no idea how this book would unfold, yet an inner voice reminded me to trust the process and this is what I did. My sense of urgency to write the beginning resulted in my first chapter on the ingesting of my unique identity—the origins of my eating disorder, the issues that have sadly infused so many of my years. At least, though, through my reflective prose, I accept their origins, and today possess self-acceptance and compassion for my damaged childhood soul. The chapters have unfolded as I told more of my story, one page at a time, never fully knowing what was to come, yet I listened to my voice, the one that demanded, *Write your truth.*

Finally, and with great reverence to this incredibly challenging work, this is the legacy I dream of for all of us—to live complete lives despite our souls' broken wings. We can repair and strengthen what was taken or lost in the quest to reclaim our self-confidence, self-esteem, and self-worth and to live a more satisfying life, one filled with acceptance and gratitude. I view my own journey as one in which others can relate, perhaps not to my unique set of circumstances, but in the realization that, whether a replacement child or not, we can polish our selected, unique memories to carry with us for the rest of our lives.

Chapter Nine
Open Doors

Follow your bliss and the universe will open doors for you where there were only walls. —Joseph Campbell

When I was younger, I often stood in front of closed doors and felt the towering walls envelop me; I was engulfed by my limitations—low self-esteem, self-confidence, and self-worth. I twisted and turned myself into the child my mother needed and expected me to be, resulting in my arduous, long struggle to own my unique inner strength as a wife, mother, daughter, friend. A gift of my passage enables me to actually view these doors, now open, as doors of growth, which might have existed all along if only I had been prepared to walk through them. Today these open doors reflect my lessons learned and self-acceptance, all hard-earned joys.

I am hopeful that many of my readers can relate to my struggles and my ultimate emotional growth. While you might not have been born specifically to take the place of another who died, there are many reasons why we view ourselves as less than, put ourselves last, feel as if we don't deserve what we truly want. With introspection and reflection, and the desire for wholeness, our lives can be fulfilling and complete with pleasure and serenity.

How, then, did I strengthen my self-confidence, when for so long, I lacked a belief in myself? How did I regain my self-esteem, which had disappeared while putting everyone else first? At what point did I see myself worthy, worthy enough to demand what I deserve—what we all deserve?

As I have previously reflected, I have always been on a quest for self-betterment, first in college with various self-help groups that popped up during the 70s—EST, encounter groups, past life regression, group therapy. What has always helped me the most, though, is my tireless examination of the pieces of my life that didn't quite work and then committing myself to change. My excellent therapist, during my early motherhood years, pushed me to reflect on my trepidation, my sadness, and my feeling of utter aloneness despite a loving family and dear friends. I feared that I, too, would mother behind closed doors and retreat to my bedroom. He explained how my mother's unresolved grief from the loss of her child could cause a lifetime of guilt and depression. He helped me to see that my mother's suffering had become my own and that she had perhaps her own terror that I, too, might die. He also enabled me to see that, for whatever reason, she connected with and preferred males. I spent hours in my head, instead, with daunting and upsetting questions, so with his guidance, I slowly picked up my broken pieces and learned to formulate the answers.

As my children grew and busyness took over my daily routine, I stopped therapy and read metaphysical literature, underscoring my belief that I needed to learn from my challenges in this lifetime so that I could evolve spiritually. With teenage children, I returned to formal guidance, and for almost a decade, I worked with a Jungian therapist, who helped me to further analyze so many of my choices and how to assume responsibility for the changes I needed to make.

When we sought drug recovery options for our son, we were introduced to yet another therapist who specialized in addictive issues as well as family systems. This dear man has carried me beyond middle age, where occasional sessions are now more for touching base and fine-tuning my growth and internalized skills. It is this psychologist who reminds me that I have freed myself from the emotional braces that limited me for so much of my life. He also gives me the credit for doing the often uncomfortable, hard, but necessary work to become whole.

I read Julia Cameron's *The Artist's Way: A Spiritual Path to Higher Creativity* and spent several years working through the book, first as part of a three-month weekly class on recovering creativity by addressing our limiting beliefs and other challenges. I then continued working through the chapters by myself for another two years. As I addressed the guided questions, my reflective responses empowered me to return to graduate school for my doctorate. The assigned activities and my honest answers also inspired me to focus on the only person I could really change—myself.

Through my entire personal quest toward serenity, I accepted my flaws, some of the personal characteristics that might have served me well when I was young, yet as an adult limited me in countless ways. Perhaps my little-girl people pleasing helped my mother to feel better, as I was determined to make her smile. Who doesn't like an agreeable person, someone willing to bend to the force of any wind? Yet, I paid a heavy price. Whenever I fall into old ways—trying to please someone above myself, especially one who doesn't deserve my caring ways, I suffer; countless times I have permitted myself to be taken advantage of, to feel used and unappreciated. That is my part and today I see this so very clearly.

People pleasing is also a quality that does not translate well into motherhood, for children are not supposed to like every decision made in their best interest. But, for so long I tried to please my boys, doing what they wanted, giving them what they desired, but there were days that I couldn't satisfy them no matter what I did and my mistake was trying so hard.

Pleasing my students and my supervisors, as I have written, made me an incredibly vibrant teacher and administrator. Yet, I spent unnecessary energy on activities and unappreciative people, causing me to feel depleted and forcing me to understand that not everyone was deserving of my devotion. I learned to be discriminant with my desire to please but not before feeling resentful and angry at my inability to set healthy boundaries.

Through all of my personal work, eventually I turned such weaknesses into strengths. I created my own mantras, replacing my mother's with my own phrases that have guided me to live more fully and peacefully. Below are five insights that I have acquired from years of painful, yet illuminating introspection. I hope they will help you, too, in attaining your own life's blessings.

I Focusing on Ourselves and Our Own Needs

When I became a mother, I just assumed that motherhood meant complete self-sacrifice. What kind of mother was I if I didn't squelch my personal needs? How could I take care of my own desires when my children always came first? I deprived myself of any possible time alone with feelings of guilt for even wanting such time. I felt that only I could take care of my kids or knew what was right for them. I shopped for what they needed and wanted, marketed, kept them busy in activities; my daily routine was completely based around my children. My only time off was in the car as I drove to work and the few hours a week in the classroom. In fact, I worked nights for 11 years so I could be home with the boys; still I felt guilty that I was leaving them even for those few hours when they were in the loving and very competent care of their father.

As I have written, despite their mother's need to suppress her own needs, fortunately, my sons are well aware of their own. Really, it was not until I was middle-aged that I learned what my sons so naturally internalized—to take care of themselves; to be good to themselves. One family event became the catalyst for my personal change.

My husband and I and our three children were at the Los Angeles Airport, awaiting a 9:00 a.m. flight to San Francisco for my niece's wedding. Michael, who at the time was 28, asked me if I had a granola bar, as he was hungry—a very simple question based on the knowledge that I usually carried everything in my purse . . . a left over practice from the long ago days of diaper bags and anticipated snacks for family trips. Traditionally, my purse was filled with gum, candy, water, protein bars, but this time I had only one bar—one I put into my purse specifically for me.

We were traveling within civilization, no deserted island, for this quick trip to Northern California. Most important, my sons were all adults with easy access to the plentiful food at the various restaurants and stores within the terminal. At that moment, I made a decision not to give my bar to my son; I wanted it for myself—maybe not right then, but at some point that day. This experience evolved into a metaphor for my personal growth, a reminder to focus on my own needs. Of course, initially, my few seconds of internal conversation were less than productive:

> *My Guilty Voice:* Barbara, give Michael the bar. He's your son and he wants it. You are his mother so you should provide for your child. What kind of mother are you?

> *My Developing Self-Worth Voice:* Yes, but he's not ten. He's almost 30. He can buy one himself; in fact, if I want, I can buy him one. But, the bar in my purse is for me. Whether I give it to him or not, I am still a great mother.

Of course, Michael knew nothing of my thoughts and did not hesitate to purchase some food once I told him I didn't have anything for him. In fact, I even told him I did indeed have a bar, but since I only had one, it was for me.

Many might find this scenario not even worth mentioning, something trivial, ridiculous even, yet it became the turning point in my own life of focusing on myself and validating my own needs. The Granola Bar metaphor symbolized my own growth. I could say 'no' and still be a good mother; I could take care of myself first and know that my adult son was going to survive without starvation, for he could provide for himself. The earth was still spinning on its axis and I could eat my own bar—or not. Even when I reread this scenario, I am embarrassed that something seemingly so trivial created such anguish, yet at the same time, I acknowledge how far I have come and how gentle I must be with my past, tormented self.

My remarkable therapist, the one who helped put our family back together so long ago shared a family story that has stayed with me and relates quite well to my Granola Bar epiphany.

His grandmother was his family's matriarch, a traditional Italian grandmother, her kitchen filled with homemade breads, pastas, sauces and her heart with maternal love, strength and goodness. For each of her family member's birthdays, she prepared a traditional Italian cake. After the candles were blown out, she cut the large, round spongy cream cake into enough pieces for everyone at the table. She cut the first piece, and put it aside, for that was always hers.

Not only was I raised to believe that the mother was the last person to get a slice if one remained, I also grew up with the "burnt toast syndrome." This idea refers to willingly accepting the rejects. Literally, when making toast for the family and a piece was burned, I was taught that the mother was supposed to take the burned piece, herself, and give the 'perfect' pieces to everyone else. To take the golden, rather than the blackened, was selfish, but it really wasn't. It's taking care of oneself first, knowing that you can then take care of everyone else as well. Today, I choose not to eat the burned piece.

I share these stories, hoping that you can also use the Granola Bar, Italian Birthday Cake and Burnt Toast stories as symbols for your own growth. Wanting the best for ourselves is to respect ourselves, enriching our own lives and then, without feeling deprived or resentful, we can more healthily give to others. It is similar to the flight attendants' safety directions regarding our oxygen masks. We are always taught to put on our own masks first and then assist others. Thus, we can first provide for our own needs and voice our desires without fear of others' responses.

Change is never easy; often our actions happen first and eventually our thinking can change, which I refer to as 'acting as if.' We can 'act as if' what we are doing feels normal, feels right when in the beginning it really doesn't. The more we repeat these actions, the more natural they feel until they become part of who we are. The following are some questions that have guided me in my quest to honor my own needs. I encourage you to write the answers and read them, not right away, but a few weeks after you have completed your responses. You will experience much illumination and clarity after the metaphorical dust settles:

1. What do you want for yourself personally (stronger self-esteem, self-confidence, self-worth)?
2. What would an interaction (between a friend, family member) look like if you had strong self-esteem?
3. What would you do differently today if you had more self-confidence? Why?
4. What or who is stopping you from acquiring these strong personal qualities? Why?

5. How would your family and friends react to your decision to grant your own needs first?

6. What do you fear about honoring your wishes and then helping others?

7. How would a typical day unfold if you could focus on yourself?

II Rewriting Our Life's Scripts That Do Not Serve Us

As I have written, I grew up not feeling good enough—second best at most things. It doesn't matter if this was true; my perception became my reality and I carried this belief into almost all areas of my life, my default position. As a result, as I have described in this book, I overcompensated by working twice as hard as a wife, mother, daughter, and friend. When I fell short, determined by my own set of ridiculous standards, I continued to feel less than. I expended much more energy than I needed for the same results.

Why did I have to make the entire dinner from scratch? Why did I tell my guests not to bring anything when their additions to my menu would have been welcomed and would have greatly helped me in my workload? My internalized script mandated that I had to do everything myself in order to feel worthy. I had to prove to others that I was the best, yet as I mentioned, I was really proving this to myself. So, another lesson I share is to rewrite our life's scripts that do not serve us, to help strengthen our self-esteem, that little voice within reminding us that we are worthy no matter what.

These are some of the questions that helped in the process of changing my outdated scripts, my internal conversations and limiting beliefs:

1. If you feel as if you aren't as good a parent as _____, what does she/he do that you do not? After you have listed what that person does, ask yourself this question: By doing this, in what ways do you think you would become a better parent?

2. If you feel as if you aren't as good an employee as _____, what does she/he do that you do not? After you have listed what that person does, ask yourself this question: By doing this, in what ways do you think you would become a better employee?

3. If you feel as if you aren't as good a family member as _____, what does she/he do that you do not? After you have listed what that person does, ask yourself this question: By doing this, in what ways do you think you would become a better family member?

4. If you feel as if you aren't as good a spouse/partner as _____, what does she/he do that you do not? After you have listed what that person does, ask yourself this question: By doing this, in what ways do you think you would become a better spouse/partner?

5. What are ten activities that you do well?

6. Why do you feel you do them well?

III Expectations are Planned Disappointments

My dissatisfaction has often stemmed from my expectations of others and of situations I could not control. I became disappointed when such expectations weren't met and most of the time, they weren't. I expected my children to act a certain way or my husband to anticipate my needs without even telling him what they were. While I have expectations of myself, of what I say and how I behave, I have worked tirelessly to remove my expectations of others, for they are out of my control and make me unnecessarily unhappy.

While I love to give, and I try never to give with strings attached, I want to be thanked and to be appreciated. To me, this is simple, common courtesy. Yet, there are those whose gratitude goes unspoken. I have to let go of this expectation; all I can do is to make sure that when I am given something or someone does something nice for me, that I am appreciative. I have no control over another's response.

In a similar way, I also make the mistake of expecting others to think and act as I do. I want to check in with my sons more often than they want to talk to me. Yet, realistically and understandably, they have their own lives and are busy making a living and involved with their families—everything I dreamed for them. When I eliminate such expectations, I am so much happier. Such expectations are "Kodak moment" versions of what I want, but this is not reality. In letting go of such expectations, I am happier and more focused on taking care of myself.

I ask myself the following questions that help me let go of such expectations:

1. How do you feel when another person falls short of your expectations?
2. Where did your expectations of others originate?
3. Who in your family has expectations of you?
4. What are these expectations that family members have of you?
5. What expectations do you have of some of your family members?
6. What expectations do you have of your spouse/partner?
7. Are the expectations you have of others realistic? Why or why not?
8. What are three expectations you have of yourself?
9. Are the expectations you have of yourself realistic? Why or why not?

IV Not Giving Advice Unless Asked

I used to freely give advice, suggestions, mandates, even. I often believed I knew what was best for my loved ones—adult children, husband, friends—and told them so. My comments began with *You should*:

>   *You should stop worrying; stop smoking; try that plumber; cut your hair.*

Of course solicited advice is different. If someone asks my thoughts about their hair, for example, then they want my opinion. But I didn't realize that I wasn't often asked. Since I stopped giving uninvited advice, I realize that few people actually ask me for my opinion, certainly my children rarely do.

That means that for a long time, I was sharing my thoughts when no one really wanted or needed them. In a sense, I was forcing my will upon them and was proud to do so, feeling as if I were "saving" them from something.

Why did I do this? I actually thought that advice was warranted and required as the role of wife, mother, and friend. I grew up with the word 'should' in most sentences. My mother began most of her sentences with this word:

You should wear that dress; watch what you eat; date that boy; live near me. I was even advised: *You shouldn't feel that way.*

I thought it was natural and necessary to inflict one's will on another, especially when love was involved. I am not referring to the mother of young children when stating the obvious: You shouldn't play in the streets; talk to strangers; play with sharp objects. I am referring to the advice given to other adults when not even asked for such pearls of wisdom.

So, how different is my life now without sharing my 'shoulds' with others? Very calm. I listen more and talk less. My own growth occurs within the silent spaces, never the clatter, and certainly not in the directives forcibly placed upon others. Now, a conversation with one of my sons unfolds in this way:

He laments:

"I have work to do, but I'm tired, so I'll do it tomorrow. My clients won't care if they get the work a day later."

My response: Silence. Or...

"I know you will make the right decision for you."

My demeanor? Calm and peaceful.

When I used to give advice, this was my response:

"You should get your work done today and then you can

rest. If you promised your customers that you would do the work, you need to do it. How can you enjoy your day off if you know you have work to do?" Then, I gave him a 'lesson' on priorities.

My demeanor? Frustrated, upset, angry, and agitated.

My son's valid and understandable response to my unsolicited advice:

"Don't tell me what to do, Mom. You don't know how I feel. You don't know my customers or whether they care when the work gets done. Just because you do your work before you rest, doesn't mean I have to do the same. We aren't the same people. I'm different than you."

The interaction caused us both to be upset with each other. The damage was done. Unless I apologized, our interaction became yet another reminder of why he would choose not to share anything with me the next time. Plus, I lost my serenity in this interaction.

I have learned that I don't have the right to inflict my will on another. How do I know what is best for anyone else—even my own adult children? It is presumptuous of me to believe they need my advice. Only they know what works for them just as I know what works for me. Today, I give others the space to make their own decisions and in this huge transformation, the underlying message reminds them that they have the tools to make the best decision for themselves. If they don't, then, they will learn a valuable lesson. We do not learn lessons from someone else telling us what to do.

Here are some questions to help you think about the seemingly "helpful" advice that you might be giving:

1. How do you feel when someone offers his/her opinion to you when you haven't asked for these thoughts?
2. Why do you offer your own suggestions when they are not solicited?
3. What are some comments you could share with someone instead of advice?
4. How do you feel when you give advice to someone?
5. What would you rather do? Listen or talk? Why?

V Gently Taking What is Ours Without Waiting to be Offered or Given

Through my interactions with my mother, I learned that I could not safely share with her many of my emotions or my differences of opinion. She did not tolerate my 'crossing her' which meant to argue or even ask for clarification, for then, she would consider me disagreeable and greatly disrespectful. When she was angry with me, I melted inside, just melted.

My subjugated voice, my acquiescence in our interactions, carried over into my exchanges with my husband, my children, my friends, my colleagues—everyone. If someone argued with me, or proved strong in their convictions, I easily gave in and then gave up, for I could not build an argument that I was never prepared to defend.

As I aged, however, I recognized that my endless submissions provided few benefits. A perennial pushover, one who responds in silence, is not endearing, and my growth and maturity depended on verbally protecting and defending myself.

At first, awkwardly, I responded with my very raw emotions, all negated through others' logical discussions. Then, I went to the other extreme, allowing my increased volume and hysteria to provide my defense. Eventually, though, I came to state my feelings; to disagree with respect; and finally to tolerate this rather messy and uneasy process of owning my voice. I am grateful for this extended lesson of self-approval, which was born from the unsteady foundation of my existence. My younger years forced me to substantiate my presence so frequently that such efforts became part of the fabric of my being.

No more. I am free of the burden to justify myself, to take what is mine, to ask for what I want, all gifts of this inward passage. I make my feelings known. I tell others what I want and need. How can they know what I want unless I tell them? If I wait for someone to give me what I want, often I never get it.

As I mentioned, when I was a newer wife, I used to expect Paul knew what I needed and wanted, what I was thinking. It never really worked, for he always fell short of giving me what I wanted. I was setting him up to fail and in the meanwhile, I wasn't getting what I wanted. A lose-lose situation.

Today, I tell him exactly what I want and he understands. He either agrees or disagrees, but at least I am my own advocate. I want to take myself away on a two-day writing retreat. Just me. My old way of thinking was:

Why doesn't he know that I need to get away? Why doesn't he suggest that I take myself on a writing retreat? Doesn't he understand what I'm feeling? Doesn't he appreciate my need to be by myself and write?

These questions and my attitude created divisiveness in our relationship. Resentment built, for I was waiting for Paul to take care of my needs—needs of which he wasn't aware. When I first mentioned that I was going to go away, he wasn't thrilled. He responded:

"When do I get to go away?"

I was not defensive in my response or filled with guilt for doing what I wanted to do because I deserved this gift of time away. Instead, I validated his feelings:

"I know you would like to go away. You can whenever you want."

That was the end of our discussion. He understood and I made my situation happen for me without waiting to be given the opportunity.

I have been taking myself on these writing trips for five years. Now, he hugs me, wishes me a great two days, misses me when I am gone and can't wait for me to come home. If I had waited for Paul to tell me to go on these trips, I would have waited forever along with an unnecessary build up of five years of resentment.

Asking for what I want and taking it has not been easy. I expected others to just know my needs, but that was distorted and irrational thinking. How could anyone really know what I want and need? My writing through this issue has shed light on my own desires and these questions can help guide you, also, in owning your own voice and taking what you rightfully deserve

1. What stops you from asking for what you want?
2. When you speak up for what you want, how do you feel?
3. Why do you expect that those closest to you know what you are thinking and feeling?
4. Do you feel there is someone stopping you from having what you want in life? Who? Why?
5. What do you want in life right now that you don't have?
6. Who is emotionally responsible for providing for you? In what ways?

VI Twenty Years From Now...?

In my younger years, I focused on unimportant issues, punctuated by worry and anxiety. My perfectionist attitude and fear of making mistakes forced me to assure everything was in order, often making unimportant events a priority, for I was concerned about how my life looked to others. I am not proud of my focus, but it is the truth.

My very nervous and anxious mother and grandmother spent an exorbitant amount of time worrying. I, too, worried about countless issues: what others thought about me; my weight; irrational fears of loss; my social life; school. My paternal grandfather, Papa Joe, once commented on my anxiety by reminding me:

"Fifty percent of what you worry about will not happen and the other 50% will happen whether you worry about it or not."

His words helped me with my little-girl concerns and as I aged, this simple phrase has helped me to prioritize my own life through an internal dialogue, which enables me to ask myself important questions. When my boys were young, such a question provided clarity as to my choices. My young son wanted to play a game with me, yet I really needed to empty the dishwasher and make dinner. I asked myself:

Twenty years from now what will be more important? The time I spent with my son playing the game or emptying the dishwasher and making dinner?

Of course I knew the answer. This question has always put many of my issues in perspective, strengthening the importance of my flexibility. I also used to reflect on the same question at work, with my students.

Twenty years from now what will be more important? The lesson I give on writing a Thesis Statement or the time given to a past student who comes by the classroom to say hello and share his graduation plans with my current students?

Clearly, my students can always use a message of motivation given by a peer, a role model.

At this point in my life, I rarely have to ask myself such a question, for I have internalized what is meaningful in my life, what satisfies. I don't agonize about issues I cannot control and more readily focus on those people and activities that provide me joy and fulfillment.

Asking yourself this question can take several formats, but you can rewrite it to relate to your own challenges and decisions:

1. Twenty years from now, what will be more important? My clean house or a visit with a friend?
2. Twenty years from now, what will be more important? Playing with my child or making dinner?
3. Twenty years from now, what will be more important? Lunch with a friend or doing errands?
4. Twenty years from now, what will be more important? Taking a walk or cleaning the house?

I hope that some of these lessons that have given me such clarity in my own life can benefit you as well. While we are all different, we seek our own versions of tranquility. In doing so, we can appreciate our unique journeys, which for me has become more magnificent than the destination. I value and accept that I could not have arrived with such splendor without my replacement-child legacy. We all come into this life with our strengths and challenges and these very elements create our ultimate, unique magnificence when we are brave enough to reflect on them.

In addition, the following books have enriched my personal journey in recovering the many qualities that had at one time been buried within a little girl who sought approval and significance. Today such literature is a welcomed friend whose valuable words provide comfort and beauty.

Socrates' words also continue to guide me: "An unexamined life is not worth living."

A House of My Own by Sandra Cisneros
Man's Search for Meaning by Viktor Frankl
Many Lives, Many Masters by Brian Weiss
On Death and Dying by Elisabeth Kubler-Ross
Siddhartha by Hermann Hesse
The Alchemist by Paulo Coelho
The Little Prince by Antoine de Saint Ezupery
The Four Agreements by Don Miguel Ruiz
When Breath Becomes Air by Paul Kalanithi
Devotion: A Memoir by Dani Shapiro
The Replacement Child by Judy L. Mandel
Replacement Children: The Unconscious Script by Rita Battat
      Silverman & Abigail Brenner, MD.
Unorthodox by Deborah Feldman
The Secret of the Soul by William L. Buhlman
Codependent No More by Melody Beattie
The Artist's Way by Julia Cameron
Lovingkindness by Anne Roiphe
Writing is My Drink: A Writer's Story of Finding Her Voice
      (and A Guide to How You Can Too)
      by Theo Pauline Nestor

And, finally, a poem by Wendell Barry "I Go Among Trees and Sit Still" reflects much of my personal journey of illumination and acceptance, as I molded my challenges into strengths.

"I Go Among Trees and Sit Still" By Wendell Barry

I go among trees and sit still.
All my stirring becomes quiet
around me like circles on water.
My tasks lie in their places
where I left them, asleep like cattle.

Then what is afraid of me comes
and lives a while in my sight.
What it fears in me leaves me,
and the fear of me leaves it.
It sings, and I hear its song.

Then what I am afraid of comes.
I live for a while in its sight.
What I fear in it leaves it,
and the fear of it leaves me.
It sings, and I hear its song.

After days of labor,
mute in my consternations,
I hear my song at last,
and I sing it. As we sing,
the day turns, the trees move.

Acknowledgments

I began and completed this book at my favorite Santa Barbara B&B, The Simpson House Inn. I am forever grateful to the large balcony that welcomed my laptop and me and where we both spent countless hours. Thank you to the staff, who with every visit, encouraged me to keep writing; they fed my soul and my body. It was there that I first met Lauren Sullivan, whose *Life Choice Retreats of Santa Barbara* provided a strong writing foundation for what was to be this book. Before her, Ronda LaRue's three-day private Soul Salon through *Ojai Soul Arts* enabled me to envision myself as healthy in mind, body, and spirit.

I am grateful to so many who have believed in me as my words evolved into pages. Claire Gerus, my original editor and now my agent, was one of the first to say, "You should publish this. It's *that* good!" Her expert guidance led me to Lisa Hagan and Beth Wareham, of Lisa Hagan Literary and Books, whose keen skills continued to shape my story and provided my book a warm, inviting home. Thank you for having faith in my writing and in me!

Abigail Brenner, M.D. took me under her wing, asking me to be a part of her most recent book's seminal research on replacement children. Thank you, too, for writing the Preface of my book. I also acknowledge fellow replacement child and author, Judy Mandel, who kindly shared her time with me.

I am grateful to so many loved ones whose positive influence and devotion are woven into the fabric of these pages. Many of my dear friends agreed to read passages and drafts of chapters, generously providing their caring feedback. I so appreciate you: Amy, Carol, Carrie, Cynthia, Darilyn, David, Denise, Emily, Iris, Liz, Lori, Louise, Martha, Mary, Nancy, Ona, Susan, and Suzanne. To Marion and DeDe, who always believed in me and my writing long before I did. They never got to read this book, but I couldn't have written it without their guidance—both physically and in spirit!

To my forever-best friend and sister Marilyn, and my cherished niece Jill—for reading with empathetic eyes, acknowledging our shared family history. To my brother Steve, who lovingly accepted my need to write my story, quite different from his own.

I am grateful to my Aunt Mary, my mother's sister-in-law and my role model. I don't believe she has ever spent a day in bed despite life's challenges. Her graceful, positive attitude demonstrates to me yet another way to grow old, without regrets—just acceptance for what is and a love of life.

To my children Michael, Amy, Brian, Allison, and Adam—for asking, "How is the book coming?" and tirelessly rooting me on when my writing days became months and then years.

To Emma, the loving, fluffy constant in my life, who also inspired my writing. When she wasn't warming my lap, she lay on the floor next to me rhythmically breathing to the tapping computer keys.

And, a profound appreciation for my husband Paul, who has taken this journey with me, never letting go of my hand while patiently waiting as I developed into the woman I was meant to be.

Finally, to my parents and to my brother Jeffrey, whose life stories unfolded as they were meant to.

Made in the USA
Monee, IL
26 May 2024

58964025R00115